Adventures in Income Property

Bert Levi

ADVENTURES IN INCOME PROPERTY

ACKNOWLEDGMENTS

A book like this doesn't come about in a vacuum, and a number of people played a role both in the words you read and the philosophies and outlook that characterize how it was written. The list is exhaustive and there's no way for me to note everyone but I want to specifically acknowledge the tremendous help from my wife Gloria and our daughters Sophia and Sarah. I want to thank Rabbi and Mrs. Ezagui of Chabad La Jolla as well. My parents, Eddie and Rosa Levi, are (and have always been) extremely supportive. Thanks to all my employees and associates and thank you as well to Jerry, who helped me organize my thoughts.

ADVENTURES IN INCOME PROPERTY

ABOUT BERT LEVI

Bert Levi has decades of business experience focusing on relationships people have with each other. He cares about relationships and the things important to them. His work in real estate continues that perspective, this time with a focus on the relationships people have with places. In fact, he became a real estate agent for that reason. For Bert, his family always comes first and he lives with them in La Jolla, California. If you'd like to reach Bert, you can email him at BertLevi@gmail.com or you can call him at 619-227-6201. Bert is an agent with Lloyd Realty Group. DRE#01897519 DRE#01802687

INTRODUCTION

I wrote this book because of the encouragement I received after publishing my first book, Adventures in Home Buying. That book focused on the ways people relate to their homes. The real estate business is, of course, far larger than just homes and I thought exploring relationships in regard to property investment would be an interesting idea. If you read my first book, you already know I have always found people and relationships quite fascinating. For most of my life, I have been in the jewelry industry and that has given me the coveted privilege to play a small role in a great many relationships as I provided engagement rings, wedding bands and gifts for special occasions.

Just as in the jewelry business I care more about relationships and people than gold and diamonds, I care more about relationships in real estate than anything else. I thought exploring the relationships people have with each other and places was a good idea and I'm thankful my first book was well received.

In this book, I'll again be exploring relationships in regard to real estate but this one will focus on real estate investments. Once again, I should make sure you understand this is not a typical real estate book. This book won't give you all the information you need to invest in real estate so you will need to do a lot more reading if that is your goal. I wrote this book to talk about people, how making investment decisions might make them feel.

There is a disclaimer at the beginning of this book but let me add to it here. Under no circumstances should you rely on anything in this book as complete information or even as information directly relevant to your situation. Real estate investment isn't something a story can express completely. You must get professional help in many circumstances, especially because almost every property investment has legal or tax implications. Please keep that in mind when you read.

I put these stories together because I believe stories are a great way to share ideas and concepts. In fact, storytelling has been a teaching tool for as long as recorded history. It is my sincere hope that some of what I write will get you to think about options that might work for your family and your particular situation.

Perhaps you will see a situation similar to yours.

Perhaps you will recognize one of the opportunities discussed in a story as something you have seen before.

I hope the stories here will inspire you to ask the right questions and think about the situations that might be right for you.

THE STORIES

Table of Contents

Monetizing Your Own Home

Celeste and Chris Decide on a Duplex

In college, Celeste studied accounting and that got her interested in business. Chris studied business and he was naturally very interested in accounting. It did not take long before the two of them realized they were interested in each other! On the day they graduated, Chris proposed and Celeste was happy to throw her arms around him and agree to be married. They lived in an apartment and worked hard. In a few years they had work experience behind them and enough saved for a down payment. So, they decided to start looking for their first home. It was Celeste who made a strange suggestion. She learned that when a person buys a duplex, they can usually qualify for first time homebuyer loans if they plan to live in one unit. She did some research and ran the numbers. She determined with her husband that they could have their home and the rental of the other unit would take care of most of the expenses. They talked about it being a first step in a strategy that could involve owning many rental properties in the future. So, their course was set, and in three more years when Celeste announced to Chris they would soon have a new addition to the family, they got to enjoy the exciting work of looking at the finances from their nine rental units to see what kind of new home they would buy for their growing family!

Tip: Sometimes, it really makes sense for a first home to be a duplex. Here are some things to consider.

1. Duplexes are multi-family homes. They are classified as homes which means you can get traditional financing for them in most cases as long as you plan to live in one of the units.

2. In many cases, the rental of a second unit can produce enough revenue to offset almost all of the expenses of the home including mortgage, insurance, taxes and maintenance.

3. Make sure, if you decide to go this route, that you consult with a professional in regard to taxes and financial planning.

A Unique First Home

Bernard came from a working-class family and his mother and father instilled in him the need to work hard. Their motto was that you should enjoy the rewards of your labor but never let yourself get in debt to support a lifestyle. They taught him frugal living and they taught him to be careful with his finances. When he met Gabby, he learned she was from a different kind of family altogether! Her parents both owned their own businesses and believed in being entrepreneurial. That meant taking a lot of financial risks and sometimes it meant periods of time when money was tight. Of course, as often happens, these two opposites fell in love. When they married, Gabby wanted to get started on some business opportunities. Naturally, Bernard just wanted to just work and be careful. When they looked at homes, they just could not agree but then they found a home that seemed like it was made just for them! The front of the lot had a nice, modest home that would work for them even when they had a few kids. That appealed to Bernard. They could buy the home now and live there for many years. As for Gabby, she loved that there was a guest house in the back along with a small studio apartment. That meant she could make the house make money for them! It was conservative for Bernard and entrepreneurial for Gabby!

Tip: Although real estate investing has risks, it is usually the least risky kind of investment. When you combine investment property with your primary home it gets even better.

1. A primary residence has benefits with taxes, financing and legal protections. Even if you have some rental units on your primary residence land, you get those advantages.

2. One of the advantages of a few rental units at your home is that you get the chance to learn how to be a landlord without a dramatic obligation of time or resources.

3. Oftentimes, homes are built with casitas, garage apartments or other extra units. Sometimes, these are added after the home is built. There are more homes available with rental units than you might think.

How About Some More Pie?

For Keri and Pat, the most important thing in their lives was pie. Keri grew up making fruit pies in her parents' bakery and Pat worked at the shop from the time he was in Junior High. Naturally, they fell in love, and when the time came for him to propose, Pat hid the engagement ring in a piece of apple pie. The two were a sweet and lovely couple, as sweet as the pies Keri baked. They went to college together and had their wedding the day after graduation. They knew two things. First, they wanted to spend the rest of their lives together. Second, they were going to open a bakery just as soon as they could. They never imagined they would be able to get started right away! For a wedding present, their parents gave them enough money for a down payment on a house. As they searched, they came across a property that had a little house in the front and a little storefront up against a busy street. They checked with their lender to see if they could qualify and they could! Before too long, they had their lovely home set up and pies galore in the cases of their new store. There were two things you could be certain about. First, the two were in love. Second, if you drove by, you would be sure to smell pie! In a few years, they had to move the bakery to a bigger place and they learned about another advantage to the property. They could rent out the storefront and make some money from it!

Tip: There are many properties that are mixed use so they have a commercial or office purpose and can also serve as a residence.

1. Keep in mind that your lender might have different requirements for a property with commercial space.

2. Remember that commercial leases are usually for longer periods of time and require more expertise.

3. If you have a passion like Keri and Pat, do not hesitate to find a property that helps you enjoy your passion.

The Rent Pays for the Mortgage!

Tom and Linda got some surprising news. Tom's annual bonus was going to be spectacular. In fact, they were pretty sure it would be enough for a down payment. Linda immediately started researching and on a happy Saturday, they visited home after home in neighborhoods they loved. One home caught their eye. It had a lovely backyard for the kids, plenty of space and a kitchen to die for! It had a nice, big great room and even a small office. There was even a pool! There was one thing, though. The garage had been converted into a studio apartment and above the garage was a small two-bedroom apartment. They did not need the space at all. Everything else was perfect, though, so they did some research. With rents in the area, it seemed like a good idea to buy the house and rent the extra units. They were delighted to discover their plan worked. A month after they got their keys, they already had a young couple in the two-bedroom apartment and a college student in the studio. The best news of all was that the rent they collected would pay for the mortgage on the house. That meant they would be able to really save and plan for their financial future!

Tip: Sometimes, renters can cover the cost of a mortgage or at least a portion of the mortgage so it makes sense to include it as part of your decision on a home.

1. Remember that you will be responsible for taxes and insurance so be sure to set money aside even if the rents pay the mortgage payment.

2. Chances are it will not be a good idea to buy a property just because of the potential rent income. Remember, your home will be more than just an investment.

3. When rental income from extra units pays your mortgage, why not set most of the money aside to build your economic future?

Carrie's Plan for College

When Carrie was accepted to the college she really, really wanted; there was a big celebration at her house. Her mother and father were overjoyed for her even if she was a bit wistful because Trina would be almost nine hours away. They looked over the numbers and realized the cost of staying in the dorms was very, very expensive. It was Carrie who came up with the idea to just buy a house. After all, the cost for just the first year in the dorms was almost as much as a down payment. Naturally, her parents were not immediately on board with the idea but later that night the two of them sat down and worked out some numbers. Even with Carrie's scholarships and financial aid as well as their savings for college, the cost in the dorm would make things tight. On the other hand, if they took the money they had set aside and bought a house, Carrie's scholarship and financial aid would cover the rest and she probably wouldn't even need to get a student loan. Even better, they could rent out the rooms Carrie would not use. That would not actually come close to paying the home off. In the end, they decided it would be the right course of action and Carrie was really surprised when her parents decided they would provide the mortgage so she could buy the house in her own name! She was well on her way, and all it took was looking at housing a little differently.

Tip: One of the best things parents can do for their children is to help them understand what it means to be on sound financial footing, and real estate investment can help. Keep these things in mind.

1. Being a landlord can help a young person learn important skills in the world of business and also help educate them about income, expenses and investment.

2. In a case like this, it is critical to plan for problems with filling vacancies. You should always be prepared to handle the cost of the mortgage even if no rental income comes and you should make sure to save some of the rental funds for contingencies.

3. Work the numbers. The average cost of staying at on campus dorms in the United States is between $8,000 and $13,000 per year. Would that money be better spent on a home? If the numbers work, it may be the wisest course.

Keeping Grandma Close

When Shelia and Frank decided they needed a bigger home, they got to work right away. The children were all bigger now, and they thought it might be better for them to have their own rooms. It was their youngest daughter Kara who said in her sweet and chirpy voice that she thought they ought to make sure they have a room for Grandma. Frank thought that was a great idea. His mom wanted to be close to family and maybe it was the perfect time. So, when they started the search, they flew Grandma in and she was involved. They were very excited when they came across a property with a guest apartment in the backyard as well as a studio apartment above the garage. Frank's mother said she would love to rent the place in the backyard and they could rent the apartment above the garage. It was a done deal although Frank and Shelia would not let Grandma pay any rent! She had a few tricks up her sleeve, though, and saved every rent payment and when she was able to announce she had started a college fund for each of the kids, everyone was amazed. Kara was proud as could be. After all, the whole idea of keeping Grandma close came from her!

Tip: Sometimes it makes sense to buy a home that has separate living quarters in order to keep family close. Here are some thoughts to consider.

1. Always check with an estate planner or financial advisor before making decisions that might affect retirement income!

2. Discipline is sometimes the most important quality. Think of it like how Grandma saved the money she would have spent in rent so she could do something important to her. Being disciplined with savings can really pay off.

3. Remember that when you think of your house as a home, you will want to be surrounded by people you love, and family and friends could be the perfect choice.

Converting the Pool House

Martha and Richard loved the house. It was just about everything they wanted. The only real issue was the backyard. There had once been a pool but it had been filled in years ago. An old pool house lay in disrepair in the back. They decided they would submit an offer that also included demolition of the pool house. Then Martha got an idea. The pool house had a bathroom with a shower. It had a game room with an old rickety pool table and a large room for pool supplies and water toys. It seemed to her they could fix the place up and add a kitchen and it would be a nice little one-bedroom apartment in the backyard. Their twin daughters were leaving for college but if they ever wanted to come back, the pool house apartment would be perfect while they got on their feet. In the meantime, they could rent it out. Martha knew a coworker was looking for a place to live. It seemed like it would make a lot of sense and the great news was they were able to still get a credit because of the disrepair on the pool house. That meant the purchase took care of the cost of rehab! All in all, things looked great, and six months later when Martha's coworker moved in, she was excited to know one of her close friends would be nearby all the time.

Tip: If you always keep your eyes open for opportunities, you will be surprised with how many come your way.

1. One of the best things about real estate is that there are often opportunities disguised as problems, like a pool house in disrepair. Think about what you can do with a property and it might open your eyes to great deals.

2. Remember that when there is a unique situation like the one described above, you will need to confirm with your lender about what options are available to you.

3. Do not forget that when you own the home, you will be able to make the decisions about how you use your property. If you can make a little extra money to help offset costs, it might be a great idea.

Her Starter Home Is a Four-Plex!

Vicky had been a renter for nearly ten years and she was really tired of not being able to make decisions about paint, landscaping and other things. She decided it was time to get a place of her own, and her husband agreed. Plus, both kids were almost five years old now, and it seemed like a good time to get to a neighborhood they might like a little better. Vicky immediately got to work and came up with a number of properties to view. On the way to meet the real estate agent, though, they drove past a small apartment building and saw a sign that said it was for sale. They mentioned it to the real estate agent in passing and he made a quick call. They had not intended to but they ended up viewing the property, and when they did, Vicky decided she really loved it. It was not actually an apartment building. It was a four-plex with four townhomes in a row. She was delighted they each had three bedrooms and she loved that they each had a private yard. In fact, each townhome was actually bigger than some of the starter homes they viewed earlier. Working with a lender, she learned a four-plex is treated as a home sale which meant she could get first time homebuyer's financing. She and her husband jumped on the idea and it was not long before they moved into their new home…and their first investment property!

Tip: Duplexes, triplexes and four-plexes are great opportunities for starting out in real estate investment because they can provide income and a home at the same time. Here are some things to keep in mind.

1. Although you will own the property, keep in mind your tenants have rights and some decisions you make about landscaping and parking might have a negative impact on your ability to attract renters.

2. Check with your lender to see how rental income influences your loan. Usually you are able to count a percentage of the rents in the qualification process.

3. Check with a tax advisor. Owning a multifamily home has tax benefits on both the homeowner side as well as the investment side. Your tax advisor can help you navigate those things.

A Four Bedroom House for Just the Two of Them?

Quinton and Kally were made for each other. They met in junior high working on the school play. Of course, the play was Romeo and Juliet, and of course both of them played the lead! Unlike the Shakespeare tragedy, though, these two were not star-crossed lovers at all. In fact, they were childhood sweethearts and they remained sweethearts in high school and college. Nobody was really surprised when they got engaged and everyone thought they were the cutest couple. Their wedding was beautiful and they worked together on their dreams, especially focusing on living within their means so they could buy a home. When they had enough saved for a down payment, they were amazed to learn just how much buying power they really had. In fact, they were able to buy a very nice home. They found one they loved but it was much too big for them! Kally got the idea they could rent some rooms to students. After all, Quinton was a speech coach at the local community college and not a week went by where they did not have gatherings of students at their apartment. It was a plan, and six months mater, Quinton and Kally had to admit it was a success. It was such a success that they started looking for another property they could rent to students.

Tip: Sometimes, renting a room can be a great way to get some extra income from your home. Sometimes, the perfect home is too large for your family but still might be a good purchase! Keep a few things in mind.

1. If you rent a room, it usually comes with kitchen privileges and some common area access. You do not have to make that the case but you will attract fewer renters if they are required to stay in their rooms all the time!

2. Keep in mind if you have tenants you will not necessarily be able to put off little repairs such as minor leaks and wall patches. These are things you might work around if it were just you but when you have renters, you have additional obligations.

3. You will want to talk to tax advisors and legal advisors. There are rules and laws you will need to follow if you have renters and you do not want to inadvertently break any.

A Cabin for the Holidays

George and Hannah grew up in the same small town. In fact, Hanna was literally the girl next door and George couldn't even begin to express how much he loved her. She loved him too and they loved their shared history. In fact, they visited home often but that eventually presented a problem. Their little town was in the mountains and it was very near a popular ski resort. That meant several times a year, the hotel prices were horrible! It really was not a problem in the beginning because they could stay at one of the parents' houses. Now, though, their siblings were older, which took a lot of space, and George and Hannah had two kids of their own. It just was not practical to stay at any relative's house. They could not afford to spend thousands of dollars on hotel rooms every year, though. What could they do? It was Hannah who found the solution. She suggested they buy a cabin they could rent out by the week for people who wanted to ski and use the rest of the time for when they visited home. She even did some research and learned there was an agency who would rent the cabin out for them. The biggest surprise was that it was highly likely the cabin rents would cover all the expenses! The other great thing? Now that they had a cabin, they found themselves visiting their family even more often and that was priceless.

Tip: Sometimes, it makes sense to buy a property you might not use all the time, especially if there is a demand for that kind of property for rental. Here are a few examples.

1. Cabins. Often, cabins are excellent choices if you regularly visit an area. Though they may be vacant for much of the time, high rents in the right seasons can more than make up for it.

2. Homes in cities you visit regularly. It might make sense if you visit a particular city for several weeks over the course of a year to buy a property instead of spending that money on hotel costs. Some business-people do that and rent the home but reserve one room for themselves.

3. Many online services market a home or a cabin like a hotel room, allowing you to rent a property to travelers who might otherwise stay in a motel or hotel.

Investing in Single Family Homes

Stephen's Accidental Investment

A marriage can be wonderful and still occasionally have situations where wires get crossed. That was what happened to Stephen and Sylvia. They were looking for a house and really loved two of them. They finally agreed on one and Stephen called the agent to make the offer. It was only after the offer was accepted that they realized they made the offer on the wrong one! They were under contract and it was for the wrong house! It was their real estate agent who suggested they see if they could buy both houses. Perhaps they could rent one out. Stephen and Sylvia had never considered anything like that but since Sylvia was an accountant and Stephen was a financial planner, they certainly had the skills to try to figure it out. They analyzed the numbers and in the end, Stephen learned the home would pay for itself with the mortgage payments, taxes and insurance even if they could only keep it rented for eight months of the year. They discussed it at length and since they had intended to use money left over from a down payment on investments and savings anyway, they decided to give it a shot. That accidental investment was the first. Five years later as they signed the closing documents on their ninth property, they decided it was absolutely worth it. If it kept up, they would be able to pay for their kids' college no matter how expensive it got!

Tip: When determining if you want to rent out a house, there are many things to keep in mind but here are some basics.

1. When determining if getting involved in rental property is a good idea for you, it may be wise to seek counsel from a financial advisor who can help you determine if the investment will help you with your goals.

2. Remember that you will need to account for your mortgage and insurance costs as well as property taxes. These are hard costs that will come out of your pocket if you cannot get rents to cover them.

3. Often, even breaking even on a rental property is a good idea because you slowly gain equity as the rents pay down your mortgage. Again, speak with an advisor.

Rachel's Relocation and Rental Decision

When Rachel got her promotion, she realized she would want to move closer to her work. The hours would be longer now, and her commute was already about forty-five minutes. So, she got to work and found a great house that she knew would be perfect for her and the kids. She knew they would especially love the big backyard. She made the offer and then did some research about selling her first house. She learned the market was not very strong in her neighborhood. She could sell the home but it would not be as much money as she had expected. Since she had other funds to use for a down payment, she did not have to sell the other one so she decided to keep it. The rents in her area were high enough that it would allow her to pay the mortgage and make a little bit of cash flow. She figured she could keep that up, and if the market got better and it made sense for her to sell, she would. It worked out really well for her. It worked out well enough that she bought another home to rent a year later. In six years, she had eight properties and she could not believe how it had all started because of a bad real estate market!

Tip: Sometimes when you move to a new home, the market makes it sensible not to sell but to keep the old home and get started with rental income.

1. This is a decision you will want to think long and hard about. Try not to make an emotional decision but consider the numbers from a distance. If the numbers do not make sense, selling the home for less than you expected might be the right decision.

2. Remember that a property that cash flows positively, enough to pay the mortgage, taxes and other expenses, is really immune to the ups and downs of the market because if the bills are paid, you do not have to worry about what the sale price might be.

Nancy's Neighborhood Choices

When Nancy decided she was going to get involved in rental properties, she did a lot of research. One thing she realized very quickly was that if she really wanted to build an income, she would need to look at areas far away from where she lived. The houses in her neighborhood were simply too expensive. The rents would not necessarily pay for the mortgage, and she was certain she would not be able to cover the mortgage herself if it was vacant for several months. She almost gave up the idea of rental properties altogether but someone suggested there were great neighborhoods in a town about two hours north of her home. She had not considered getting properties so far from home but she took a leap of faith and did the research. Boy was she glad she did! She ended up discovering a lot of great opportunities and when she finally chose a neighborhood, she realized she could get three different homes with the budget she had set aside. It required thinking about things in a different light but she was happy she had an open mind about it because three years later she had almost eleven properties and everything was working out fantastically! All it took was thinking outside of her comfort zone and being open to trying.

Tip: If you are going to invest in rental homes, you are going to need to do some research about neighborhoods. Here are some thoughts for you.

1. It is easy to fall in love with a property. For your home, that is a great idea. When it is a rental property, though, you need to think differently. For rentals, the most important issues involve the numbers, not the beauty of the property.

2. Depending on where you live, it may not make sense at all to buy single family homes in your neighborhood in order to offer the house for rent.

3. You can get help from a property management company if you decide on properties a distance away.

Dana and Charlie Think of Their Future

They were still young, only a few years out of college. They had dated from the first semester, though, and they had made plans for years so right after their honeymoon they put a budget in place and focused on saving. They were able to buy a home and a year later they realized they liked the frugal lifestyle enough that they had saved more. When they talked about how to invest their savings, Dana suggested they look for rental property. Charlie said he would give it a try but he had never considered it before. They looked around and narrowed it down to four properties. They picked one and Dana worked the numbers. By her calculations, if they got a ten-year mortgage, the rents would cover the cost. Then, in a decade, they would own the property free and clear and they could sell it for a very nice boost to their retirement plans. They bought the property but things did not go as planned. That is because they were so happy after a few years that they got more rental houses! By the time that ten years passed, they would not have dreamed of giving up one of their rental properties. Instead, they enjoyed the cash flow and continued to build their future day by day.

Tip: Rental homes can be a very good option for young investors. Here are a few reasons you might want to consider a plan like Dana and Charlie.

1. Although it is usually a much better idea to invest for cash flow than for equity, every month your rents will still pay down the mortgage and that is a big advantage.

2. Do not forget that there are tax benefits such as appreciation that also come when you own a rental property.

3. Remember that if you take any steps toward your financial future that involve large expenditures, you should probably talk to a financial advisor for advice and feedback.

Ellie's Eleven Houses and Counting

Ellie and her sister Hazel had always been very close. People often confused them for twins even though Hazel was a year older. Nobody was really surprised that when they married, they had a double wedding. It also surprised nobody that they bought houses right across the street from each other. They were a little bit surprised, though, that Ellie focused on investment while it did not seem to interest Hazel at all. Ellie bough her first rental house three years after she and her husband bought their first home. She bought another a year later and the third year, she bought three! That was five houses and she decided to try for two a year. She was faster than that. Five years after she started, she had eleven homes. That was when Hazel finally decided she wanted to get involved as well. Of course, Ellie was happy to help. As far as she was concerned, there was plenty of opportunity for everyone. Ellie had eleven houses and used all the profits from her rental property to pay off her primary home's mortgage faster. She could not wait to sit down with her sister and find out how she would use the money she earned.

Tip: The truth of the matter is that most of the time, the key to success is just getting started. Here are some ideas to keep in mind.

1. No investment is perfect. The real key to success is to make the decision to begin! That does not mean be rash but it means you will never find a perfect investment without any risk. Searching for it can just paralyze you.

2. Once you get started, you will likely get very motivated to do more. This is why getting started is so important.

3. Remember that "getting your feet wet" will have a greater impact on all you want to learn than anything else possibly could.

Linda and Bobby Rent a Home

When Linda's company relocated three states away, moving was not really an option. It would mean all of the kids would have to change schools and Bobby would have to re-sign from his job. After a lot of discussion, she decided not to follow the company made the most sense. She got a nice severance package and that was when she got the idea that maybe she could start her own business. Bobby thought it was a great idea but what business should she start? She thought maybe she could try out real estate and so she and Bobby looked at a number of homes and finally found one they thought would be a good choice. They made an offer and when it was accepted, they excitedly put it up for rent. Years later they would laugh at themselves. They did not really know what they were doing, and they made a lot of mistakes along the way. In the end, though, it was all worth it because the learning experience from that first house made the next one easier. The next one, too. The next one, too! It was the start of a new journey in their lives and Linda never looked back with regret at her decision not to move with the company. Her bank account was happy, too!

Tip: For some people, rental properties is a small way to earn extra income. Some people, though, treat it like a business. Here are some ideas for you.

1. If you are going to run your investments like a business, that means you will want to make yourself accountable just like you would if you had a boss. You do have a boss. It is you!

2. Running a business means you need to make decisions based on good criteria and not emotions. This means you will pass on houses you might like but which do not make sense.

3. Remember you have customers! They are your tenants and it is important that you treat them with customer service in mind.

Can Jason and Chris Get the Whole Street?

It started out almost like a joke. Jason and Chris decided they wanted to get started in income property investing and they both started researching. They were surprised when they sat down in the evening and discovered they had both settled on the same neighborhood. The same street, in fact! The house Jason found was just a few down from the house Chris found. The first thing they considered was that the two houses in the same place confirmed the numbers they had both independently analyzed. The second thing they considered was that maybe it made sense to go ahead and buy both houses. It was not the original plan but they had the credit to get the loans and they were confident the homes would offer cash flow above and beyond the cost of the mortgage. Their original plan was to make a sizable down payment on one home. Instead, they made a reasonable down payment on both. It worked out better than expected and, of course, it did not take long before Jason began bringing up the possibility of buying another property. Would you like to guess where their next home was located? Just six houses away from the first two. At that rate, they thought in ten years or so, they might have the whole street! It was a wonderful goal and who knows? They will probably make it.

Tip: Learning about a neighborhood and determining if it will work for you is an important aspect of rental home investing. Here are some thoughts for you.

1. What works in a neighborhood for cash flowing properties may look very different than the neighborhood you live in. Do not be blinded by standards you expect in an upscale area.

2. Some investors choose to buy their properties in only one or two neighborhoods. This allows them to come to an understanding about an area and improve as they go along.

3. Be careful because if you focus only on one area, you are exposing yourself to the risk that particular area might see a downturn.

Winne and Michael and the Three Bedroom House

When an uncle passed and left Michael his home, he was not sure what to do about it. He appreciated the gesture but he had only met the man once! His mother told him that was just the way his brother was, and Michael and his wife Winnie went to take a look at the property. It was very nice but with four kids and Winnie's home business; it was not the kind of place they could use. They considered selling it but then Michael decided to check on rents in the area. It seemed like it would be a good idea to rent it rather than sell it. It was free and clear after it cleared the estate. After several months, they realized that made a whole lot of sense. They saw cash on a regular basis from the rents and they were learning a lot about real estate. The next year, they took out a mortgage and used the money to put a down payment on another property. That one worked out as well! A decade later, they realized they could retire at any time. They had lived frugally and investment their money in house after house and their properties generated far more money than their salaries. Sometimes they had a hard time believing it all came from one three-bedroom house! It just goes to show that sometimes getting started is all it takes to make a big change.

Tip: Because rents ideally take care of the costs of purchasing or owning a home, it can be much easier to scale up investment with rental homes. Here are some things to consider.

1. You can use equity from one property to provide a down payment on another property. You will want to be careful you do not have a mortgage payment that is bigger than the rent!

2. Remember that big success is the result of several small successes. Be consistent and work toward your goal to see the results you would like to see.

3. Above all, focus on each property not just the day when you might have several. Each property needs to make sense.

Lisa and Nathalie Learn to Let Go

One of the hardest things about investing in rental properties for Lisa and Nathalie was realizing that they would not enjoy some of the neighborhoods or metropolitan areas where the investments made sense. It took a very skilled real estate agent to help them understand that people need homes no matter their economic station and not everyone enjoyed the kinds of high-end things they enjoyed. He explained that for many people, a good hot dog from a street vendor was better than a pastry and a latte. She agreed to give it a shot and before long, they had a property in mind. It seemed to make a lot of sense and so they entered into a contract and got started. Over the years, the two of them still sometimes had to come to terms with the fact that they were investing in areas they would not live themselves but they loved that they were able to provide quality housing for people and they loved that they could do that. Sure, they were more comfortable in their own neighborhood with the corner coffee shop and the little bistros but that did not mean the neighborhoods where they invested were not great places others would enjoy. In fact, some people really and truly preferred them. They never would have though investing in real estate would open up their eyes to other things! They certainly never expected their real estate investments would make more money for them than their salaries, but that is what happened, and they could not be happier.

Tip: Home bias is an investing concept that explains people tend to think their immediate area is the only good area for investing. Keep these things in mind.

1. If you want to invest in rental properties, you probably already enjoy a pretty good standard of living. It can be easy to think a home is too small or has too few amenities. Remember that not everyone has the success you enjoy.

2. Without real estate investors and developers, there would not be single family homes for people to rent! Do not forget that being a landlord provides a service people really need.

Ralph and Sunny Buy a Home

For years, Ralph made extra money by running a lawn care company on weekends. He only spent two mornings a week on it but it led to a very nice savings. One day, he noticed right on the lawn he was about to mow was a sign. The house was for sale. He immediately knocked on the door and was surprised to learn the person living there was a renter and not the owner. He asked if he was moving and the gentleman said he did not want to move but would probably have to find a new place when the house sold. Ralph thought about it later that evening and spoke with Sunny. They had a nice savings. What if they were to buy the home and continue to rent it out to the gentleman already living there? Would that not be a good way to make their money work for them? Of course, he had to make sure the numbers worked, and that was when Sunny really came in handy. She was the member of the family who really knew money. She helped determine that they could not only manage the purchase but that it would be a really good idea. Armed with that knowledge, Ralph made the purchase. Of course, the renter was very happy he did not have to move, and Ralph and Sunny were happy, too!

Tip: You can oftentimes buy rental homes that already have a tenant in place. There are some things you will want to consider in those cases.

1. Unlike multi-family properties, a renter in a single-family home does not usually impact the price of the property.

2. Remember that in order to invest in a home you really want to make sure that the numbers work. Do not fall in love with a home, a situation or a neighborhood and then make poor decisions. Make sure the numbers work!

3. Remember that with any substantial investment you may want to consider speaking with a financial advisor to see how the investment fits with your financial goals.

Investing in Multi-Family Homes

Stan and Esme Buy a Duplex

There was no doubt about it for Esme. She had read book after book on the subject and she wanted to invest in real estate. Stan thought it was a good idea but he wanted to balance the investing with other forms as well. He thought some stocks and bonds, some precious metals and some other investments should be part of the mix. Esme would rather they spent it all on property! The two worked out a compromise. Instead of trying to work out how to buy the twelve-unit apartment building Esme had her eye on, they would buy a duplex and work out the kinks before trying a bigger project. Esme was excited and wanted to jump in on everything right away but she agreed that it probably made sense to take something smaller on first. As for Stan, he was overjoyed. He was always restrained and Esme was always energetic. Together, they always seemed to come to the best decisions and he could not imagine what he would do without her. The next day, Esme presented seven different possibilities and they settled on one that had an extra garage just so he could use it for storage. They were excited. Working together and using both of their strengths gave them an important first step. That is really what love is all about, is it not?

Tip: Real estate investment can be part of an overall investment strategy if you want to maintain diversification. Keep a few things in mind.

1. You do not have to buy real estate with cash. One of the wonderful advantages of investing in duplexes or triplexes is that you will in almost all cases use a mortgage for the purchase. This allows you to make larger investments with less cash.

2. As you learn the ins and outs of income property investments, it probably makes a great deal of sense to start with a smaller property and tackle larger projects after you have experience.

3. Do not fall into the trap of believing only one investment is appropriate. It is okay to use a measured approach with real estate or anything else.

Barry and Amelia and Three Units for the Price of One

Barry and Amelia decided when they learned they would soon have their first child that it was time to get serious about their finances. They both liked the idea of real estate and since Barry was a contractor and Amelia was studying to be an architect, they thought they would probably be good at it. They were a little disappointed when they realized all of the single-family homes in their area would not cash flow positively. Amelia was ready to give up. Barry suggested they look at duplexes or triplexes. Amelia felt skeptical. After all, would not a triplex cost the same as three houses? It just seemed like it would not make any financial sense at all. Still, she agreed they should at least look, and boy were they surprised! It turned out the triplex was not the cost of three houses! In fact, the three-unit multifamily home was so close to the cost of a single-family residence in their neighborhood that it was almost like getting three homes to rent for the price of one. Naturally, they jumped on the opportunity. It was an exciting and significant moment and Barry and Amelia were overjoyed. They knew they had taken an important step in ensuring the little one growing inside of Amelia would have a great financial start! Life was beautiful for this lovely pair.

Tip: Often, multifamily homes have a far smaller cost per unit than single family homes. Here are some things for you to think about.

1. Multi-family homes usually qualify for attractive home financing, which makes it easier to purchase them.

2. In general, the cost per unit (a duplex has two, a triplex has three, etc.) is significantly lower than the cost for a house. In fact, in some areas, a four-plex may cost less than a single-family home!

3. As with every other real estate investment, the key is for you to make sure the numbers work. If a property cash flows and provides a reasonable rate of return, it is a great investment to consider.

Happy Students and a Good Deal for Krystal

When Krystal went to college, she rented a room from a family just a few blocks from the college. When she and Dale married and moved to a college town, she wondered if it made sense to do the same thing. They were not as close to the college as the family Krystal rented from had been, though, but Dale thought there was still an opportunity there. The next weekend they drove around the college and looked at various neighborhoods. They even found a property for sale. They ended up choosing a different property in the end, though, a triplex. Two of the units had three bedrooms and two had two bedrooms. That meant they would be able to rent to ten students. The numbers seemed pretty good. In fact, even assuming the rooms were all vacant in the summer, they would still make money. Dale suggested they could offer a discount during summer months and that might even encourage people to take classes during the summer semester. They decided to go ahead and buy the four-plex and that started them on their grand real estate rental property adventure. A few years later, they "graduated" and purchased another four-plex. They felt excited and knew they were definitely on their way to real safety and security.

Tip: Oftentimes, renting to college students can be a profitable venture. There are definitely some thoughts to keep in mind if you decide on this course of action, though.

1. Remember that college students tend to be less reliable than other renters. This can impact your cash flow.

2. Remember there will be additional work if you rent room by room instead of the entire unit. There are also obligations to each room renter individually. Make sure you seek advice from a professional.

3. Do not forget that you will likely face summers or other times of year when your property is not very high in demand at all. You should plan for the lowest vacancy rates to be during normal semesters and the lowest during breaks.

Julie and Xander Get Their Duplex!

When Julie and Xander married, they were just out of college and they rented half of a duplex as their first home together. They enjoyed it there but also wished they had their own home. Julie used to joke that someday she would own the duplex. Six years later, they had their own house with a beautiful backyard for their two children to play and plenty of space for Rusty, their lovely rescue German shepherd, to run. One night when they talked, Xander mentioned he saw a sign at the duplex. It was for sale! The very duplex they rented when they were first married? It seemed like such a romantic and beautiful thing, like a sign from the heavens. They immediately made some calls and learned they could definitely afford to buy it. They had never really invested in real estate before but it had always been something they planned to eventually do. They figured it was a good time to get started and they made an offer on the duplex. Only after they had committed to the purchase did they realize they did not actually do any research. There was a lot of panic as they tried to make sure the property would work but it turned out they were fine. There were renters already in place and their rents would cover all the expenses and give them a small profit. They were relieved and very happy. They had their duplex and they were sure that over the years they would probably buy many more though none would be as special as their first!

Tip: Remember above all else that real estate purchases are very personal. Sometimes, particular properties are special to us. Here are some ideas to keep in mind.

1. Yes! It is okay to buy a property because it has sentimental value to you even if it does not necessarily make as much money as another property might. However, be very careful not to buy a property that costs you money.

2. One thing about which you will need to be careful is to remember that a property, even if nostalgic, is an investment. You need to make sure of it from an investment perspective, and that means analyzing the numbers.

3. One of the most important things to avoid is allowing love for a property to drive you to impulsive decisions. They are risk and do not always work out like they did for Julie and Xander.

A Beautiful Four-Plex for a Beautiful Couple

Marilyn and Edgar were the picture of love. When they became high school sweethearts, everyone thought they were
very cute. When they stayed sweethearts in college, everyone realized they were serious. When they were married,
everyone thought the wedding was beautiful and more than
one person felt a little bit envious about the way they looked
at each other and clearly loved one another. They were
sweet and beautiful together, and that made them very special. They both worked very hard, and that was another
thing that made them special. They worked hard and lived
within their means, focusing on frugality and making sure
that they saved as much money as they could every single
month.

Tip: When you are ready to take on the challenge of a multi-family home it is important to determine the impact of vacancies on your decision. Keep a few things in mind.

1. While a vacant unit in an apartment building is a small percentage of the total rent, a vacant unit in a multi-family home can represent anywhere from twenty-five percent to fifty percent of the income.

2. It is always a good idea to have some funds saved from the rent every month to build up a reserve in case of unexpected contingencies or simply to cover the mortgage is there are vacancies.

3. Above all, remember that it is always a good idea to seek advice from professionals, especially if you find yourself unsure or unclear about any of the criteria you have set for purchase.

Paula and Kendall Decide to Try

For Paula and Kendall, decisions came slowly. They were both very deliberative and made sure they analyzed something from all possible angles. Perhaps the only time they did not do that was when they got married. They were sure from the very beginning that was the right decision. Now, almost ten years later, unhappy with the performance of their stock portfolio, they decided they needed to consider other options. Naturally, real estate was one of the possibilities they discussed, and it did not take long to decide it was a better option for them than other possible investments they might do. But how would they get started? They talked to a number of people about it and did a lot of research and finally came to the conclusion that they should choose multifamily properties. To meet their financial goals, they would need several but like most of what they did, they decided on a measured approach. That meant they would buy one for now, learn everything they could about owning one and managing it and then pick another. That was exactly what they did. They took the plunge and bought a triplex. They were surprised to learn that it was not as much work as they had expected. They began planning just a few months later for what they would do next, and after plenty of planning and evaluation, they bought two more duplexes. They never stopped the deliberate and careful approach but made slow decisions every step of the way, and they were glad they did!

Tip: Multifamily homes are a great way to get involved in rental real estate. Here are some thoughts for you to consider.

1. Maintenance of a property will be your responsibility, and you need to account for that in terms of cost, time and effort.

2. Financing for multifamily homes is often very attractive because they fall under the "home" category in most areas from a legal and a mortgage sense. This can often mean better terms, which means better cash flow for you.

3. Renters are usually more consistent and take better care of property in a multi-family home situation.

Audrey and Nick Get a Property

When Audrey and Nick got married, they decided right from the outset to be very frugal and careful with money so they could accomplish their dream and buy a house. They were surprised with how quickly they were able to do that, and on their fifth anniversary they realized their frugal habits led to a nice savings balance. Since they already had their home, they talked about what they ought to do next. The first thing they decided was to go on a nice second honeymoon. Their first honeymoon really did not involve much, and they knew it would be important to build memories. After the honeymoon, though, they wanted to get started on building a financial future, and they had already discussed buying a duplex or a triplex across the street from the factory at which Nick was foreman. They enjoyed their second honeymoon and built a great many memories and when they came home, they took their first step on building a secure tomorrow. They looked as six different properties and chose a duplex. They were excited and hoped in the next several years to buy many more. With the factory going strong, they knew there would always be secure renters. The two of them enjoyed a nice dinner out after closing, something they decided they would do every time they bought a property. It would make eating out even more special than it already was. Frugal living had really paid off and Audrey and Nick knew this was just the beginning.

Tip: Frugal living can do more for your financial wellbeing than you can possibly imagine. Living within a budget can help you to save the money you need to pursue your dreams.

1. Wealth has a lot more to do with what you spend than what you earn. Live within your means and save money. You will be surprised with how things grow for you.

2. Sometimes savings is easier with a goal but more than anything, savings is a habit. Put ten percent of your check away every single payday. You will be glad you did.

3. Most of the time, our money is spent on convenience after convenience. You should avoid that as much as you can. Make your coffee at home and pack a lunch. Eat dinner at your own dining room table.

Charles and Jennifer Fix It Up!

For some time, Charles and Jennifer noticed the triplex once a week. They drove by it on their way to visit Jennifer's grandmother every Saturday morning. They always had a brief conversation about how it was sad that the place was empty and in disrepair, especially with such high demand for rentals. One Saturday morning, Charles said, "Maybe we should just buy this thing and fix it up ourselves." That seemed like a crazy idea when it was spoken out loud but after their visit with Grandma, they went to lunch and talked more about it. It would be a wonderful thing for the neighborhood and if they could just break even with it, they would still be building equity in the property for the long-term success. It seemed like a good thing to do. So, they went to a real estate agent and asked her to help them find the owner and see about a sale. It took a while but she finally discovered the owners and negotiated a purchase for them. The couple were overjoyed. In a few months they were working on the property and three months later it was good as new! The same real estate agent was also a property manager and she took care of finding renters. Things were wonderful and every Saturday when they drove past the property, they felt absolutely fantastic for how that property was transformed. It was exciting. It was special. It was the first step for them on the road to financial freedom, too!

Tip: Sometimes a multifamily home that needs repairs represents an excellent opportunity. There are a few things to keep in mind.

1. This works very well if you have some understanding of construction and handyman work. You can use those skills to protect and support your investment.

2. In many cases, obtaining financing for a property in disrepair is difficult. It often follows a different path than a loan for a property that is ready to go. Be aware of that and realize your cash investment might be larger than you expect.

3. Do not forget that there is a great deal of work that goes into any rehabilitation of a property. Do not trick yourself into thinking it is easy!

Sometimes, You Just Go For It!

Belinda and Zane were not very impulsive. They loved each other dearly, and they always thought through everything. Change was not easy for either of them but an opportunity arose and Belinda thought perhaps they should reconsider their recalcitrance. There was a subdivision with duplexes about ten miles from their home. Sometimes Belinda's work led her to drive through it. One day she saw a few signs. Some of the duplexes were for sale. She could not let go of the idea that she and Zane should buy a property. They had talked about it for many years but never actually took the first steps. She did not even wait for the end of her shift before she called him and said that she believed they should talk in the evening. That night, she told him about the properties and even though her reacted with a bit of hesitation as she expected, she kept talking until he finally agreed it was time for them to do something different. The next weekend, they looked at several of the properties and then started working on choosing which one they should buy. Eventually, Zane said, "If we don't just go ahead and buy one, we are going to end up never doing it!" There were three properties that made sense so they just chose the one closest to Belinda's work. A year later, with four duplexes in their portfolio, they were grateful they finally just took the plunge.

Tip: The hardest thing about getting started in investing in real estate is sometimes just getting over the fear of getting started. Here are some tips.

1. Most of the time, when we experience difficulty getting started on something new it is because we have not learned enough to get to a comfort level that enables action. Take learning seriously and it will help.

2. Sometimes, we have to make a choice and more than one choice seems good. We can let that keep us from taking action as easily as we can sometimes be afraid to act because of the downside. Sometimes, action is the only cure for paralysis.

3. Keep in mind that once you have the information necessary to make a decision, coming up with new things to analyze is often just fear. If you have the decision, take action.

Hector and Lilly Invest in Themselves

When he was growing up, Hector's father always taught him to pay himself first. What he meant was that he should set aside a portion of every check for savings. Hector did that from his very first job, and his discipline was one of the reasons Lilly found him fascinating and wonderful. When they married, he shared that philosophy with his new wife, and it really paid off. They were able to buy a home for themselves right after the honeymoon. A few years later, Lilly suggested they consider buying the four-plex across the street from their home. They certainly had the finances necessary because of how careful Hector was about finances. At first, he was resistant but Lilly explained that it seemed to her having that property generating rents would be like paying himself first all the time. He could not argue with that logic and so they made an offer. Six months later, they bought another property. In five years, they had almost seventy units. All the while, they still lived frugally. Hector and Lilly were proud of themselves. They knew they were investing in themselves even while they slept. It was exciting and even more exciting because now they had two little kids. You can be sure Hector began teaching them very young that they should pay themselves first!

Tip: One of the most important things you can do is save a portion of your income every single paycheck. It could change your life!

1. We tend to spend our take home pay. The key is to think of the money you save as already out of your check. If your work allows it, having a portion sent directly to a savings account is a great idea.

2. Sometimes you can save money by denomination. For example, at the end of the night if you have any five-dollar bills in your wallet, save them!

3. You will likely be surprised that living frugally will not mean you lose out on fun and things you like. In fact, when you are not wasting money, you will be able to afford more of what really matters to you.

Investing in Apartment Buildings

The Impossible Dream Comes True

Lonnie and Annjanette could not believe it. When they bought a little rental house years before, they never thought their real estate side business would grow so powerfully. Now, they stood in front of a large apartment complex with ninety-two units. It was unbelievable but it was theirs! They had worked very hard to get to the point where they could afford such a property but they were excited they did. Now, they could impact the lives of many tenants and they could be sure their children and even their children's children would be secure. As they walked their new apartment complex, they thought back to all of the sacrifices they had made over the years. There was a lot of frugal living. There had been times they kept an old car another year so they could use the money they had saved to buy another property. They had lived frugally long after they had the means to have a luxurious lifestyle so they could continue to build their portfolio and make sure to have something that would last after they were gone. There was a great deal of work behind them and they knew there was a great deal of work ahead of them as well but there was a great deal of cause for celebration and as they looked at the apartment building that now belonged to them, they knew it would all be worth it.

Tip: Building on successes in real estate is easier than you imagine and the key is to focus on doing the next right thing to build your business.

1. Do not try to grow too fast. Just do the right things day by day to build your business. This will keep you on track and is sure to help you grow in a way you can manage.

2. If you have smaller goals like some extra income, a few rental houses might be all you need. If you have larger goals, you should seriously consider building toward purchase of apartment complex.

3. Remember that while you can manage smaller properties more fluidly, an apartment building will need to be treated like a business if you want to be successful.

Penelope Makes a Few Changes

When she bought the small apartment complex, Penelope decided right away she would make some changes. She knew just a few changes could really transform the property. The first thing she did was have the landscaping fixed and added a few barbecues. Then, she had the buildings repainted. Then, she had the parking lot resurfaced and had the lines repainted. She also added some assigned parking spaces, and that added to the building's revenue. Just those few changes already attracted a more upscale clientele for new leases and the prior tenants grew more loyal. More than anything, though, she loved walking around her apartment complex and seeing the changes she had made, changes that not only improved her profitability but also improved the quality of life for everyone involved. When she bought it, the complex was well past its prime. Now, it had a reputation as a reasonably-priced but upscale location. It did not take long before that reputation meant there was a waiting list for people to move in because there were not any vacancies! Penelope looked at the property she owned and thought about how happy she was just trying to make things a little better for everyone.

Tip: Often, the most important things you can do to increase revenue at an apartment building do not actually require a great deal of work or effort.

1. In most cases, you will have to resurface and repaint parking lots at some point. Configuring the painting with premium spaces costs no additional money but can result in more revenue. It also makes things better for the tenants.

2. Cosmetic changes such as keeping the grass mowed and repainting can make a dramatic difference in the quality of life for residents. It can also lead to bigger rents.

3. Remember that changes that are small or low-cost from your perspective may seem very big and profound for your tenants.

Roberto and Jasmine Make the Decision

After almost ten years of investing in single family homes and duplexes, Roberto and Jasmine decided they wanted to consolidate. They had properties all over the state and even though they were very happy, it took almost all of their time and effort to keep up with everything. With six different property management companies managing their properties, things could get a bit confusing. They decided they wanted to have things a bit more manageable. For them, that meant consolidating their properties into one of two apartment complexes. She was pretty sure cutting down to one property management company, one balance sheet and one profit and loss statement would save a dramatic amount of time and energy. Their research also suggested that the change would not reduce their income. In fact, it seemed it would actually earn them more. That was exciting, of course, and they went about the process of selling off their smaller properties and narrowing down their choices for the apartment buildings they wanted. It was a joy to do that. They knew they were making the right decision and they knew it would mean they could really begin to enjoy the fruits of their labors. Roberto and Jasmine went about the new direction with the same determination they had shown building to this point. Something great was right over the horizon, and they were overjoyed.

Tip: For some small real estate investors, consolidating to apartment buildings can save time, money and a lot of hassle. Here are some things to consider.

1. Managing fifty units spread out over a large geographical area is very likely going to require much more work than fifty units in a single building or complex.

2. Perhaps most importantly, when you have an apartment building, it is critical to remember to treat it like a business. Although there are many benefits to apartment buildings, running them correctly is important!

3. When you own houses, you do not have the same opportunity for revenue enhancement that you typically have with an apartment building. Learn to think along new lines when you own a complex.

Roy and Danielle and Their Tenth Anniversary

Roy and Danielle were a very cute couple. All their friends said that when they first met in high school. All their friends said that when they were in college. They said it when they married and they said it on their fifth anniversary. On their tenth anniversary party, though, everyone seemed a bit awed by them. They were millionaires! This cute couple was more than just cute! Naturally, their friends wanted to learn how it happened and Roy and Danielle told them it all started with a plan. They told them when they were in college, they bought their first duplex. At the time, they were engaged but not married. It was really exciting a year later to change the property so they held it as a married couple. They made it a goal to buy one property a year but soon discovered as they built their portfolio that they were able to far exceed that goal. In fact, they sold some of their properties and bought a little apartment building after six years. Two years later, they sold all of their houses and bought a slightly larger complex and a year later they bought another. Now, their portfolio included more than a hundred and forty apartments. Naturally, their friends were excited for them and more than one of them was excited to see about trying the same journey themselves. Their friends still all said they were a cute couple but now they also said they were a cute millionaire couple!

Tip: A common way for real instate investors to build their net worth is to take the success of their business and trade their properties up to bigger locations with more units.

1. The key is planning and discipline. Just as it can be easy to stay in your comfort zone and never invest in the first place, it is easy to just get comfortable with single family homes or multi-family homes.

2. You should speak with a tax advisor when you sell a property. In most cases, you can defer your tax burden from any capital gains by buying another property within a specific period of time.

3. In almost all cases, managing one ten-unit apartment building will be far easier and less time consuming than managing five two-unit duplexes.

Ashley and Miguel and the Dog Park

When Ashley and Miguel met in college, they both lived in an apartment complex near the campus. They thought the apartments were nice but they always felt disappointed because even though renters were allowed to have dogs, there was never a place to let the dogs run free. This was particularly frustrating for them because there were large open areas that would have been perfect. Naturally, the two never could have imagined they would buy the apartment complex as a tenth anniversary gift to each other! Of course, it had changed a little since they lived there. They hired a landscaping company to take care of the property and they noticed an immediate difference. They added a fresh coat of paint and cleared away some old appliances that were just left in a corner of the parking lot. They resurfaced the parking lot and made some repairs to the carports. And...of course! The dog park! It felt wonderful to plan it, and the tenants sure were happy. It was one of the few complexes in the city that actually allowed pets, and they were all excited. As for Ashley and Miguel, it was like a dream come true. The apartment complex was special to them and it was also proving to be a fantastic investment. For the two of them, though, there was almost nothing as exciting as watching the dogs playing in the dog park.

Tip: It is important to remember that owning an apartment building is owing a business. The tenants are your customers and delighting them is a good way to succeed.

1. Amenities such as dog parks, outdoor dining areas and barbecues can attract tenants and also keep them there.

2. Remember that when you own the apartment complex, you can make changes that are important to you. You will want to be careful to ensure they will not harm your business or cause resentments.

3. There are a great many apartment complexes out there but that does not mean you will find one that has everything you would like. You can consider as you purchase options that might make sense.

Hillary and Francis Take on a Big Deal

For a few years now, Hillary and Francis had focused on buying properties. They had seven houses and some multi-family homes. It was only natural that when a friend of theirs drove by an apartment building, he would share with them that it was for sale. They were not really interested but they decided to check it out. It seemed overwhelming. If they bought it, it would be twenty-five units all at once. That would be more rental units than their entire portfolio! Still, they had a process. They wanted to make sure that they could tell their friend they seriously considered the building so they analyzed the numbers. It was really eye opening. They realized that when it came right down to it, those twenty-five units would cost less for management, taxes and even the mortgage than all of their other properties combined. Furthermore, they saw a number of ways they might be able to make the property generate even more revenue. It seemed like a really good idea to them, and they never would have expected that. They made an offer and when it was accepted, they entered into this new world happily. They had an apartment building? It was never part of the plan but now that they had been enlightened, they were certain they would make apartment complexes a definite part of their strategy. How could they not?

Tip: If you invest in homes and then see an opportunity for an apartment purchase, you are likely to experience a lot of the same emotions as you felt struggling with the first purchases you ever made.

1. An apartment building requires different analysis than a single-family home rental but the basic formulas are the same. The rent should cover all of the expenses and also provide you with some cash flow.

2. Just as Hillary and Francis focused on small properties when they started in real estate, that is very likely the best thing for anyone getting started to do. Gaining experience with smaller properties will make larger properties easier to handle.

3. The story of Hillary and Francis illustrates how important learning to be flexible can be. It is important to have discipline but with real understanding of the processes in real estate, you can learn to recognize opportunities.

Haley and Josh and Curb Appeal

The numbers made a lot of sense for the rents the apartment building provided but Haley and Josh felt confused. The rents were far lower than the market rate for the area. Out of curiosity more than anything else, they told their agent they would like to tour the complex and when they did, they understood immediately why the rents were so low. The building desperately needed curb appeal. It needed new paint and needed better care in regard to the landscaping. There was a pool but it was empty with big signs warning kids not to play there. She wondered why in the world it had fallen into such a state. The building made plenty of money! In fact, it could make far more if the owners just treated it with care. She made an offer and when the property closed, she immediately hired contractors to get to work. In only two months, the property looked beautiful and everything was functional. With fresh paint, well-maintained landscaping, and a pool that was no longer an eyesore, Haley and Josh had a building that was a real winner. The rents went up and nobody complained at all. Best of all, Haley and Josh were excited to see that many of the tenants' kids were playing outside now and enjoying the pool. The apartment complex was a great deal and she was able to make it a wonderful place to live for the tenants. What could be better than a win for everyone?

Tip: Just as a rental home can rent for more when it has curb appeal, apartment unit rents go up when the outside is well presented.

1. Does the building need a fresh coat of paint or an updated color scheme? Does it need something as simple as mowing the grass and repairing cracks in the walls?

2. When a property appears to be old or poorly maintained, it makes it very difficult to attract renters. Fix it up to keep your apartments full!

3. When the property becomes more beautiful, you will see more excitement and activity from the tenants. That adds energy to the building and can only help you.

Audrey and Spencer Increase the Value

Audrey loved thinking outside of the box with her apartment buildings. She knew the value of the building was based on the operating income and she considered ways to increase it. First and foremost, she realized the rents were below market so as leases expired, she brought them closer to market value. Second, she realized people took their laundry to an outside location because there was only one coin washer and dryer and they were often broken. She remedied that by partnering with a company that transformed the laundry room. Finally, she worked with the utility company so the water would be individually metered. Now, she got a small percentage of every unit's water bill. She loved how the apartment building seemed to really work with economies of scale. What she loved most, though, was that it seemed like most of the changes were intuitive. Why would an owner of an apartment building not make storage units available to the tenants? Why would an owner of an apartment building not have vending machines so people could get snacks and drinks conveniently? It certainly seemed to her like the decisions were simple. She did not know why the previous owners had not done the same thing but she knew she liked the results.

Tip: Because with an apartment complex there are many units, small changes can have a dramatic impact on revenue. Here are some thoughts.

1. In a complex with twenty units, an increase of $25 per month in rents per unit results in additional revenue of $500 per month or $6000 per year. In most markets, that increases the value of the property by fifty to sixty thousand dollars!

2. Laundry services, vending machines, trash services, premium parking, storage units—these are some of many options available that can increase your revenue.

3. Remember it is always better to add value your tenants will appreciate and pay for than to cut back on those things and expect them to pay the same rents.

Woody and Belle Listen to Their Tenants

Woodrow and Belle owned an apartment building and most of the time they felt like they were banging their heads against a wall. They had worked very hard learning about real estate and bought several small properties. Eventually, they sold all of their properties and used the funds to buy a thirty-unit apartment building. It was profitable but it seemed like there were always problems to deal with. They did not know what to do and really considered selling it. Then, a friend asked if they ran it like a business. They did not know what he meant and when they did not have an answer, he asked if they treated their customers with respect. After a long discussion, they realized they never really interacted with their tenants or tried to learn what they needed. They decided to change that. They immediately set about sending questionnaires to all of the tenants. It asked what they needed and also asked if there were any suggestions. They were surprised to learn that even very minor repairs like door knobs and the like took weeks or even months to be addressed! They also learned the washing machines and dryers were almost always out of order. Parking was never enforced so it was hard to find a parking space! It was a shock to the system but they were glad to learn the truth. They immediately got to work addressing the issues and they were amazed at how much easier it was after the tenants knew they would be treated with respect.

Tip: Remember that your tenants are your customers. Often, just listening to them can make a big impact on the operations of your business.

1. Your tenants are likely to give you opportunities to make money simply by telling you what services they would like.

2. When minor repairs are left unfixed, studies have shown the tenants will be less vigilant about taking care of the property, which leads to larger maintenance costs down the road.

3. Remember that it is far more expensive to attract a new tenant than it is to keep a tenant already in place.

Oliver and Aldo Use All Their Space

When they bought the apartment building, Oliver and Aldo did everything right. They knew they could increase revenue simply by fixing the curb appeal, making sure the laundry rooms and vending areas were functional and by offering rentals of refrigerators and washer/dryer sets. Once all that was done, they still wanted to increase the value of the property. As they brainstormed, it was Aldo who came up with the idea that perhaps they ought to build some covered parking spaces. They knew they could charge for them and it would be a good service for their tenants. Then, they thought about how it would not be all that difficult to build some storage units along the side of the property. That, too, would be a way to best utilize their space. They also considered how there was a unit used just for storage. That did not seem to make sense to Oliver and Aldo. It seemed to them there was enough storage already. That was money that would not only increase cash flow but also increase the value of the property itself. They thought that was a pretty good idea! Later, they considered just how wonderful the property had worked out. It was appraised at significantly more than their purchase price, and they were happy about the changes and the positive effects. More than anything, though, they were happy they had really considered the possibilities.

Tip: There are many ways to increase revenue in an apartment building, and here are a few ideas that might get you thinking.

1. Covered parking or premium parking spaces usually do well in an apartment complex and are relatively inexpensive for the money generated.

2. Do not underestimate the revenue that can be generated by renting appliances such as refrigerators and (if you have hook ups in the units) washers and dryers.

3. The best way to increase revenue is to make the property more appealing and more valuable so that when rent increases come, your tenants will be glad to pay.

Investing in Office Buildings

ADVENTURES IN INCOME PROPERTY

Don and Diane Head to the Office... Building

For a number of years Don and Diane invested in various companies and one day Diane said, "You know, rent is always the biggest expense after payroll." Don wanted to know if she wanted them to invest in real estate leasing companies. She laughed and told him she thought they should start buying office buildings. Don thought it could be a great idea and agreed to give it a shot. They had experience analyzing businesses, and so it did not take too much of a change in perspective to analyze an office property. Like a business, it had a balance sheet, an income sheet and a profit and loss. In fact, they realized running an office building was a great deal like running a business. That was something they already understood! They narrowed down a few choices and sold off some of their positions in various companies. When they identified a potential property, they were excited about this new chapter in their lives. They had the tools necessary for success and they were committed to working just as hard on this new venture as the other projects that meant so much to them. They were confident and excited, and that was a beautiful thing for a couple to enjoy.

Tip: Office space is usually in very high demand and if, after consideration and seeking out relevant advice, you think it might be a good choice for you; here are some thoughts.

1. Office leases are far more complicated than residential leases because there are more laws to protect both sides of a residential lease. That means you will need to seek help in order to create a lease for an office.

2. With every step in the real estate process, the need to treat your properties as businesses grows so be sure to focus like you would on a business you own.

3. Remember that each kind of property in which you might invest has different requirements, different benefits and different tenants.

Mr. and Mrs. Hagen Invest Their Savings

Their friends thought it was very cute the way Jen and Bob never called each other by their first names. Right after they married, Bob called Jen Mrs. Hagen and she returned the favor. Now, almost fifteen years later, they still spoke to each other that way, and it was a great reminder that they chose to spend their lives with each other. They had been careful with money and lived frugally. They also made some prudent investments. They had not planned to get into real estate but then Bob learned that the office building where his company was located was up for sale, he had to tell Jen right away. She thought the idea was exciting and she giggled to think that he might work for a company that actually rented the office space from him! They got the analysis of the building and set about seeing if they could acquire it. It would require a large down payment but they had successful investments over the years and were pretty sure they would be able to manage that. They checked the rents and discovered the building would cash flow positively. When it came right down to it, they could not come up with a reason not to take the opportunity. Bob never told his employer he owned the building. He did, however, very much enjoy depositing the checks his management company sent for their rent!

Tip: Remember that an office building is a business all by itself. You will want to approach it as a business and run it like one.

1. Your tenants are your customers and they are by their nature businesspeople who will expect a certain level of service.

2. Unlike residential customers, there are near constant attempts to get your tenants to seek other locations. You need to offer service that makes them want to stay.

3. Remember that just like any other property, you will need to ensure that your office property makes financial sense in regard to the initial investment and the ongoing revenue.

Pete and Connie Go Executive!

When Pete inherited a small office building from his grand-father, he did not know what to do with it. After all, the offices were all small and it really did not fit with the current trend of open work places. His first thought was that he should just sell it and be done with it but Connie had another idea. When she first started as a financial consultant, she worked out of an office at an executive suite. The building might not be suited for a normal office building but it seemed perfect for that. Executive suites were interesting because they allowed people to share certain resources like conference rooms and even receptionists and clerical employees. It was for smaller business or for external offices just for, as the name suggested, executives. There was a lot of opportunity, though, and Pete and Connie enjoyed learning about how to make it happen. First and foremost, they created a corporation to own the business and to provide the other services. They did some minor remodeling and made sure there was a conference room on both floors. They created an attractive reception area and hired good staff. They had to put in a good phone system and from there they were ready to go. A few years later, they were amazed at how well it worked. They had partnered with many companies that helped small businesses and things could not be better.

Tip: Executive suites can be an excellent choice for some properties. Here are some things you will want to keep in mind.

1. Typically, you will provide certain office functions at an executive suite such as receptionist service, copying, internet and the like.

2. While you will get many entrepreneurs who represent a reliable tenant, one of the things that appeals about an executive suite is the mobility involved so keep in mind long leases are unlikely to be attractive to potential renters.

3. Perhaps the best thing about owning an executive suites office building is knowing you are helping small companies to grow and succeed. Even giant companies were once tiny!

Paulie and Xochitl Decide on an Office

They knew they wanted to own real estate but they did not really want to deal with residential renters. The primary concern for Xochitl was that she did not want to be on call late in the evening. Something that could be handled during business hours seemed a much better choice. As for Paulie, he was used to dealing with businesspeople so he thought he would rather have them for tenants. They were young, of course, so they did not have a great deal of buying power. They were able to find a small office suite with seven suites and it was a great start. After a few years of running it, they added another building, slightly larger. After ten years, they had many thousands of square feet of office space earning them a very, very nice return. It was, without question, a wonderful feeling to realize they had gone right into the world of offices. They loved being around small businesses and they loved feeling like they were a part of them in some small way. Most of all, they loved that when they went home at the end of the day, they were home! Things were absolutely wonderful, and this couple would not have it any other way.

Tip: There are some advantages with office space if you treat management of an office property as a business. Here are some thoughts.

1. Typically, you will do most of your work in regard to office space during regular business hours.

2. There are small office buildings that may be within the price range for any level of investor.

3. Not requiring off-hour attention does not mean that office buildings do not require your attention at all. Remember, an office building is a business and you should treat it like one.

Edgar and Caitlyn Buy a Building

From the time he was young, Edgar always dreamed of having his name on a building. He would see big buildings in the city with company names and logos and always thought about having a building with his name right at the top. He thought it was just a dream but as he and Caitlyn worked on their financial setting, they lived frugally and invested prudently. It was Caitlyn who first saw the office building that would eventually have Edgar's name right at the top. It was a nice three-story building and the for sale sign seemed old and worn, like the property had been on the market for a long time. Caitlyn talked to the agent listing the building and got some information. The property had been on the market for three years. Caitlyn analyzed the numbers and decided it was not selling because it was priced too high. She showed all her research to Edgar and suggested they make an offer closer to the appropriate value of the building. After three years, perhaps the owner was ready to see reality. He figured it was worth a shot, and Caitlyn could not have been happier when she saw the expression on his face when his name was installed on the building. He was so happy, and the investment was sure to pay off!

Tip: You should take pride in any property you have and if you have an office building, taking pride is especially important because it will impact the attractiveness for potential clients.

1. Always make sure the grounds are maintained and that your tenants' clients would be happy to arrive there.

2. Just like with a house or another property, office buildings need to be priced correctly in order to sell.

3. Just like with any other property, you can make an offer that is slightly or even substantially different than the terms suggested by the seller.

Love at the Office

Ariel and Jon met at the office. They did not work at the same business. They both toured an office building for sale at the same time. For a decade, Ariel had invested in properties and was ready to own a business complex. As for Jon, he owned two smaller office buildings and wanted to sell both of them to buy a larger building. They viewed each other as competitors, of course, and did not really trust each other. Of course, that is what happens when you are on opposite sides of a transaction. On the other hand, neither Jon or Ariel could get the other one out of their heads. It turned out neither of them bought the larger building but they did go to lunch to compare notes. Lunch became dinner later in the week. Dinner became a movie and then a trip to the beach. You probably know how this ends. The two were married and began searching for property investments together. There was one thing everyone in town knew. If Ariel and Jon got involved in an office building, the building would succeed. From competition and distrust to collaboration and love… It does not get any better than that!

Tip: There is opportunity for joy in this life even in the strangest places! Here are a few thoughts about what can be joyous about investing in office properties.

1. Although you may have some very large companies who rent space from you, in most cases your lease-holders will be small family businesses; and you can be proud about helping them succeed.

2. Remember that when you own an office building you are not only providing space to companies but also providing employees with the opportunity to have a job and a place to work. Take joy in that.

3. Take joy in the relationships you develop as you work on real estate. You may not find true love but you will certainly make friends and learn a great deal about a great many people.

Hal and Jean Consider Their Options

Hal and Jean were proud of their achievements in real estate. They owned a few multi-family properties and they also had partnership interests in a few office properties. They thought over the years they had learned enough to seriously consider buying an office building of their own. There were three options they really liked and each of those options was close to their home. It seemed to them they would succeed with any one of them. That was the problem. If there was one property clearly better than any of the others from an investment standpoint, they would not have had any difficulty at all figuring out which course to take. That was not the case, though. On the contrary, they knew they would be happy to have any one of the three. So how in the world were they supposed to decide? The final decision was almost silly. One of the properties had eaves that offered more shade. It was just a minor thing but with no big criteria, they decided to go with that. The building worked out, of course, and Hal and Jean found themselves wishing time and time again for decisions like that one, where everything was such a good choice picking which one to do could be difficult!

Tip: There are many office property opportunities that may be very good choices. Sometimes you need to look at more than just the numbers to see what to do. Here are some thoughts.

1. If you are comparing properties that are the same financially, you will want to determine what other factors such as location and, in some cases, just personal preference.

2. You may want to consider the tenants you might like. Are you interested in very small businesses? Choose buildings with smaller spaces. Are you interested in tech companies? Choose buildings in areas that are more "hip."

3. You may not be able to put your finger on why you like one choice more than another. It is your life. If the numbers work either way, you can feel free to go with your gut.

Dee and Vance Choose the Shell

In many cases, office buildings are unfinished on the inside. An unfinished building is called a shell. A shell allows a tenant to make improvements to a space in order to better meet their needs. This is what Dee and Vance learned when they looked at several office buildings. Vance was aware that retail space often worked out that way but he did not realize the same was true about office buildings. It was interesting and exciting and it also made sense for their goals. Vance wanted larger companies as tenants, the kinds of companies that signed three-year leases and took half a floor or more. Since he was a consultant for the financial industry, he had a great many contacts and he was certain he would be able to find tenants who would be secure and stable. He knew it would be a little less expensive than a completely finished interior and he also knew he would need to be prepared to offer credits to leaseholders for their tenant improvements. He thought it was a good idea, though, and Dee agreed to follow his lead. In did not take long to receive confirmation. Just a week after closing, a software company leased a whole floor. Dee and Vance felt great. It was a new experience but it seemed like it would work out great!

Tip: If you are going to buy an office building that is primarily a shell, there are a few things to keep in mind.

1. For the most part, shell buildings will be more attractive to larger tenants, who will want to be able to make decisions based on customizing according to their own designs.

2. In many cases, when you rent a space that requires tenant improvements, you will offer a credit for those improvements, essentially paying for the customization of the office. This makes financial sense because leases are usually longer.

3. When you invest in shell buildings, you must be prepared for a longer wait between tenants. This is why you should probably be in good financial shape before you even consider it.

Just Another Day at the Office

When Walter first considered real estate investment, he worked as a customer service representative at a small tele-marketing firm. While he worked and attended school, he considered buying houses and land. He read all he could and it was not long before he also considered other property types like mini malls and office properties. For some reason, even though he worked there every week for more than three years, he never thought about the office building where he worked. By the time he graduated college, he owned a small triplex. He lived in one unit and rented the other two to students. In fact, he met his wife when she came to see about a unit to rent! After graduation, he worked very hard, this time managing a customer service call center. Slowly, he and his wife built their portfolio and it was his wife who noticed the office building was for sale. He had not worked there in more than fifteen years but it almost seemed exactly as he left it. He knew with just a few cosmetic chang-es he could update the look and the place could be far more successful. In fact, he might be able to get his employer to rent some of the space. They pulled the trigger and six months later, Walter managed his call room in the very suite he worked in at his first job. For everyone else working meant just another day at the office. For Walter, it meant just another day of living the dream.

Tip: Just as stock investment should be diversified, you should also consider very carefully the merits of diversifying your property portfolio, especially if it grows very large.

1. A good mix of properties can be a hedge against a downturn in any specific type of property whether it is residential, commercial or office space.

2. Remember that just like a home, updating the cosmetic appeal of an office property can be an important investment of resources for overall profitability.

The Best Office Space Imaginable

Tami believed the best office space in the world would be the right choice for her when the time came to invest in office space. She had decided to invest in offices from a young age when only a block from the home she grew up in, she saw a construction site and her father explained the developer was creating an office building. She watched the construction as often as she could and loved the way it changed from just a plot of land to a nice building with windows that seemed to gleam in the sun and people in fancy clothes arriving for work every day. She was enamored and she studied very hard, taking an interest enough that her first job in high school was working for a real estate broker. She kept that job as she went to the local community college and when she finished her degree a few hours from home, she worked for a broker in her college town. She always dreamed of owning an office building just like the one she saw built when she was young but she never expected she would own that very building! She noticed it was for sale when she visited her parents on Thanksgiving. By Christmas, she had gathered together partners and made the offer. By Easter, the property was hers. She was thrilled. Her dream had come true in a beautiful way. Her parents were thrilled as well. They knew they would see her a lot more often!

Tip: Owing an office building can be an exciting and joyous thing, and it is a goal that is achievable for anyone who is ready to put in the work and do what is necessary to make it happen.

1. Do not think you should not dream big. There are great opportunities available in this world, and those opportunities are available to you!

2. You can think of real estate as simply a way to make money but how much better it will be to invest because you love the idea of creating value for people!

3. Making financial decisions that are also lifestyle decisions is not only acceptable but a very wise thing for you to do. Do not be afraid to live your dream.

Investing in Retail Space

Perry and Leah's Mini Mall

They did not know why they did not think about it before. When Perry was offered early retirement, he had a choice. He could simply enjoy himself doing nothing at all or he could enjoy himself doing what he loved, restoring antiques. His wife suggested they find some space for him in a local mini mall. He could restore antiques and sell them. He liked the idea but also thought maybe buying a stand-alone building would be better than paying for a lease. As they researched, Leah suggested they buy a mini mall and he take some of the space and lease the rest. It would help defray some of the costs and make it easier to start the business. Of course, that made it all seem a great deal simpler than it really was but with hard work and a great deal of effort, they were able to find the property, acquire it and set about making a good start for the business of antique restoration and the business of owning a small strip mall. Sure, there were a lot of learning events along the way and some of them were frustrating and stressful. On the whole, though, Leah and Perry were not just happy with the decision. They were overjoyed! The investment paid off and Perry had the chance not only to enjoy his antique restoration but to share that joy with many people.

Tip: Owning a mini shopping center can not only be gratifying from a financial perspective but it can also help a neighborhood by providing services. Here are some thoughts.

1. Just like renting a garage apartment can help defray expenses for a mortgage, renting space in a mini-mall you own while operating a business from one of the suites is a great way to turn an expense into an asset.

2. The advantage of operating a business in a retail center you own is the same as the disadvantage. You are right there at all times. You will be able to address any issues but you will not always be able to escape needing to give immediate attention!

3. It is never too late to get involved in property investment. Sure, the stereotype shows a young entrepreneur but do not believe the stereotype. You can follow your dreams no matter your age.

Gina with an Art Gallery?

Gina and Mario had a wonderful life. Mario was very successful as a business consultant. He went to companies that were failing and helped them get back on their feet. As for Gina, she was a very successful artist who only produced one or two paintings a year but each one sold for many thousands of dollars. They loved each other dearly and enjoyed their marriage immensely. The two never thought their two different businesses would interact but then the art gallery which often displayed Gina's work and sold many lithographs told her they would have to shut down. The owners had died a year before and the kids discovered they were in horrible financial shape. They had no idea how to keep the gallery open. The good news was situations like that one were exactly what Mario dealt with in his career. He took a look at the business and suggested it could be fixed with a nice cash infusion simply by selling the building. How would that work, though? He explained a leaseback meant the business could sell the property and then rent the space. The cash infusion would put them back on solid footing and the business should be able to operate effectively. The best news, Mario thought it was a great property and he suggested they buy it themselves. They got another surprise, too. The kids had no experience running an art gallery and asked if Gina could help until they found a good manager. Gina loved the chance to help them out and to honor the memory of the people who always showed faith in her.

Tip: Oftentimes, opportunities come up that we just do not expect. The key is to recognize them so you can take advantage of it.

1. Owning real estate is a great deal more secure than owning a business. Often, businesses that own their building end up selling it and leasing the property back.

2. Sometimes, companies are healthy in operations but external factors (like the death of a partner or a natural disaster without enough insurance, etc.) make it necessary to sell off assets. When you buy a retail space in those circumstances, you might just save a company!

3. This story shows that one of the most important things a real estate investor can do is be open to opportunity. Good deals come up regularly, and the key is being open to them.

The Historic Corner Store and Florentino's Commitment

Florentino and Luz loved the corner store. It was part of their childhood and they could remember way back in elementary school when the two sweethearts would walk three blocks from their house so that Florentino could buy her a piece of candy. They walked to that store in junior high and in high school, too. When they married, they bought a house close by and they walked there regularly. The store had been located in the same place for fifty-eight years but they were dismayed to learn it would not be there for its sixtieth anniversary. The owner of the building was getting married and wanted to sell his real estate as he started the new phase of his life. He already had some interest but the interest came from a large gas station chain. That meant the corner store would be torn down! Florentino and Luz owned a number of houses and he told his wife that if she asked, he would be happy to buy the building so it was not torn down. She was thrilled with the idea and they immediately went to the owners of the store and asked if they wanted to stay open. When they said they wanted their children and their grandchildren and great-grandchildren to have the company just as they got it from their grandparents and parents, Florentino said to leave it to him. Whether they believed he could help, he did. In just a week, he was able to tell them the building was in escrow and he would be the new landlord. Luz was so happy she bought a bunch of things at the store to make a special dinner. As for Florentino, he bought Luz a piece of candy!

Tip: In today's world of giant superstores and the internet, it is easy to forget that small local markets and shops are very important to neighborhoods.

1. Local shops that serve a small geographical area typically direct their products and services based on the needs of the people with whom they are intimately familiar.

2. There is a definite need for the kind of diverse, varied and exciting small businesses you will find in neighborhoods, owned and operated by people from the neighborhood.

3. Real estate investment is just like any other business in that there are opportunities to do good things and if you take advantages of those opportunities, you will be glad you did.

Channing and Carter Decide to Stay

When Channing and Carter bought their RV, they thought they would just travel the United States for the rest of their lives. Since they both worked from home, they knew they could work from their RV. They also had a number of properties that provided steady cash flow and slowly built a secure retirement for them. They did not think their excitement about real estate investing would convince them to stay in the same place! That is exactly what happened, though. In the travels, they found a small town they really loved. They knew they would return their time and time again. It was supported mostly by tourists travelling the interstate and it seemed busy and full of life and excitement. They noticed a building for sale. The building had tenants— a candy store, a small soda fountain, a tee-shirt store and a little collectibles shop. As soon as Channing looked at Carter, he knew what they would do. Of course, at he thought they would still travel but it was hard to give up the excitement of the town. Years later, they owned several of the buildings and they loved how they could encourage the little businesses that made up the character of the town. They especially loved that they were able to keep historic buildings beautiful but keep the authentic history in place. They still took vacations in their RV but as far as they were concerned, their whole life was a vacation already.

Tip: Some people enjoy investing in real estate because they love the idea of revitalizing a location while keeping its character. Here are some thoughts.

1. A fresh coat of paint does not have to mean you change the entire character of a building. Just as you might paint a classic car in classic colors while remaining authentic, you can be authentic to a vintage building's character while still making it beautiful again.

2. Remember that some places are historic but that does not mean that things have to be falling apart! Restoring a property to its former glory does not have to mean changing it from vintage to modern.

3. Some towns are filled with character and depth of history. It is wonderful when you invest in places like that and help anchor tradition and keep the "flavor" intact.

Fiona and Darryl Buy a Building

They had, for some time, thought about what it would be like to own property, and when they got their feet wet by buying their neighbor's house when he moved, they were happy with the result. After four years, they had a number of properties, and they were very happy about their progress. One Saturday, when they were enjoying a date, they walked from the little bistro where they had lunch to do some window shopping. They enjoyed the quaint neighborhood and when they saw a vacant shop with a sign that said for sale or lease, Darryl made joke about how they should buy the building. It was just a joke but when Fiona brought it up again the next morning, the idea began to settle in their minds. A quick phone call to the agent would not hurt anything… A month later when they signed contracts to buy, they felt a great deal of excitement. They were finally getting started on something they wanted to do for a very long time. When escrow closed and they owned the building, they extended their contract with the real estate agent so they could find a company to lease it. They were very happy when specialty shop that focused on imported toys from all over the world rented the space. The shop was hip, interesting and they thought it would be a great success. Life was really exciting, and they were glad they had a chance to diversify their portfolio.

Tip: Sometimes opportunities arrive just because you are going about your everyday business. If you keep your eyes open, you might be amazed at what crosses your path.

1. If you take a day to do some walking, you are very likely to notice shops and buildings in ways you had not before. Keep your eyes open and you will be amazed at what you see.

2. When you have an opportunity to take vacant property and make it useful again, there can often be a wonderful sense of accomplishment. You deserve it!

3. Just like any investment portfolio, a portfolio of properties benefits from diversification (which means having different types of investments instead of all the same type.)

The Caruso Family Owns a Shopping Center!

When Rafael decided to do something as a family, his sisters Lorna and Elena thought he meant go on a vacation or something like that. So, they were very surprised when he took them to a corner shopping center. There were a small grocery store, a coin laundry, and several other small businesses located on the spot. There was a stand-alone building that had a flower shop and Rafael teased Amelia and Elena that he had sent both their husbands there for last minute Valentine's and anniversary purchases. Why were they there? Rafael wanted them to buy the little shopping center! Naturally, his sisters looked at him like he was crazy. Sure, they had the money to do it but what in the world did they know about running businesses like the ones at the strip mall? Rafael explained that they would not have to do anything with the operations of the business. They would do some promotions to get people to come to the location because their leases gave them a percentage of sales but they did not run the businesses at all. The sisters sighed. They could argue with him but Rafael always got what he wanted! They gave in and decided they would learn all they could. Four years later, with six strip malls in their partnership, they were glad they did.

Tip: Family members and friends often pool their re-sources to buy retail properties, especially little mini-malls and neighborhood centers. Here are some thoughts.

1. Even though you may invest with family members and friends you trust, you still need to make sure you have documented the partnership. Documents that make the ownership positions and rights of the part-ners clear help avoid arguments later.

2. Remember that your tenants operate the business. As a property owner, you want to make sure you make the property attractive and do your part to attract cus-tomers but just like a landlord does not set your chil-dren's bedtimes, you do not handle the issues related to the operations.

3. It is very common to have a lease that includes a per-centage of the retail sales to go to the landlord.

Gene and Ginger Buy Their Favorite Store!

For as long as they had been married, and that was almost two decades now, Gene and Ginger loved to shop at a little specialty foods store down the block from their home. The store had lots of goods they could not get anywhere else. They stocked Cannellini beans from Italy just like the ones Gene's grandmother always used. There were tins of canned meat from England and there were oils, vinegars and cheeses from all over the world. They loved that little shop and when they learned the little street shopping center where the shop was located was up for sale, Ginger said they just had to buy it! Gene could never tell his wife no, so it was pretty much settled. However, he made sure to do things correctly, analyzing the property and the rents and ensuring the purchase would be profitable and that they could handle the management of the location. He also reviewed the lease and made the purchase contingent on the company signing a new lease on the same terms. Everything worked out, and when the property closed, they had a celebration right at the store. The proprietors already know Gene and Ginger as their best customers and now they were happy to have them as their landlords. As for Gene and Ginger, they were as happy as they could be! They never expected to invest in property this way but they were glad they did!

Tip: The great thing about little shopping centers with small businesses is they keep the character of a neighborhood alive. Big chains are wonderful but there is nothing like a corner specialty store!

1. Remember that small businesses drive the economy. Sure, there are some locations where a giant company employs a great many people but the day to day transactions in the lives of people are fueled by small enterprises.

2. The best shopping centers and strip malls are characterized by good relationships between the tenants and landlords, and that involves both sides doing all they can for the business to succeed.

3. Retail property purchases often include contingencies such as renewals of leases or other tenant actions prior to closing.

Dorothy and Kelly Like to Dance

There are many reasons people invest in real estate, and there are a great many things to consider if you want to buy a retail property. Dorothy and Kelly decided to buy their little retail building because they wanted a dance studio in their neighborhood! Their children took dance lessons, and they were dismayed when the building where the dance studio was located sold. The studio had to relocate and were an hour away now. From that moment, Dorothy decided she would find a property to buy where a dance studio could be located. She searched various locations and settled on a nice building with four suites. A small diner was located in one suite and a gift shop in another. They bought the property and Dorothy got right to work. She knew a dance studio would be perfect for one of the other two. She finished the inside of the sweet with wood flooring and put mirrors on the walls. When it was all done, she called her daughter's old dance instructor but she was unhappy to learn they had a new lease and could not move back for at least three years. She felt depressed, like all her work was for nothing. Kelly got involved then, hiring an agent to find a dance company that would be able to use the improvements already in place. When he found one, Dorothy and Kelly celebrated the only way they knew how. They went out dancing!

Tip: You can market your retail property to specific kinds of stores and services. Some mini malls are very kid friendly while others are geared more to adults.

1. Unlike a large shopping center or a mall, most strip malls and mini malls do not really need an anchor store but you do want to find high traffic businesses.

2. In most cases, you will not tailor a suite to a particular kind of business but when the opportunity arises or if part of your plan involves a specific business type, it is definitely something you can do.

3. It is a smart decision to be flexible. You may want a particular kind of store or service but it may not be something that could succeed at the location you own.

Oscar and Asa and their Strip Mall

Oscar and Asa had planned for this purchase for a very long time. They loved their residential property investments and they were nice and lucrative but they wanted to move into the world of commercial properties. They were not sure if they wanted to invest in office buildings or some retail buildings but they knew they wanted to own some property with businesses as tenants. They enjoyed working with small businesses and they enjoyed the idea that they were providing a service to them. When they saw a strip mall that clearly needed some maintenance on the buildings and the parking lot, they did some research. It turned out the mall was owned by a company on the other side of the country and when they made an offer, the company was happy to sell. Oscar and Asa were overjoyed and they immediately got to work. The tenants seemed skeptical at first. Evidently, a long line of owners had come with plans to change things and never did. Oscar and Asa were different. They closed half the parking lot and had it resurfaced and repainted. Then they did the other half. The tenants began to hope. Then, they moved suite by suite fixing up the place, repainting and making the strip mall beautiful. When it was done, the tenants were amazed and business really took off. Within a year, Oscar and Asa had potential tenants seeking them out all the time! What could they do? It was simple. They bought more properties.

Tip: When you try to decide on what kind of retail property you would like to own, there are some questions you will want to ask yourself.

1. Do you want a single tenant or multiple tenants? In other words, are you looking for a building with only one store or more like a strip mall?

2. If there is work that must be done on the building or buildings, is that something you will enjoy as part of the process or do you want to start off with everything already perfect?

3. Remember that your tenants are your customers. Upkeep of the property makes it more attractive to their clients and that allows them to pay you the rent.

Sully and Claudette Like the Corner!

When they decided it was time to see about adding a few retail properties to their portfolio, Sully and Claudette told their real estate agent to find them some possibilities. They spent almost four days from the morning until the evening looking at places but they still had not found any properties that really appealed to them. They could not put their finger on anything that was wrong with any of the properties. None of them inspired the spark most of their other property purchases would inspire. They were disappointed but they knew if they were patient, they would find the perfect opportunity. It happened about four weeks later when they went out to lunch. They wanted to try a small restaurant they had driven past a few times but had never patronized. While they were there, they noticed a space for lease. At lunch, while making small talk with the waiter, they learned the space was originally held by the owner of the building, who was leaving the country. They had never considered buying this property on the corner they drove by almost every day but they discussed it and agreed that if they had toured it when they looked at the others, it would have been their choice. They called the number on the leasing sign and expressed their interest in buying. They were overjoyed to learn the owner was open to an offer and they were even more overjoyed a few months later when they had lunch again, this time in a building they owned!

Tip: Sometimes you need to look at a great many different properties to find one that is right for you. There are some things to keep in mind, and here are a few of them.

1. Try your best not to be so excited about purchasing an investment property that you grow impatient and settle for something less than you want.

2. Keep your eyes and ears open for opportunity. It is certain to come if you make yourself available for it.

3. Just because a property is not currently listed for sale does not mean an owner will not be open to an offer. If you like a property, it does not hurt to ask.

Investing in Special Opportunities

Fixing Up the Mini Mall with Tom

When Jennifer talked to her husband about investing in real estate, he was very much interested in buying run down houses and fixing them up. To him, that was the best thing they could do, and he was certain it could result in some very successful and very lucrative projects. Jennifer agreed there was a lot of opportunity there but she was more interested in investing in properties that would generate income for them. So, he ended up fixing up a house every now and then and she slowly built their income property portfolio. One week, they drove by a little mini mall in really bad condition. There was one little convenience store there, and it seemed to do very well. As for the rest of the spaces... nothing. Jennifer made an offhand comment. They could buy that and fix it up like on of Tom's houses. Then, she could rent the spaces. Best of both worlds. She intended it as a bit of a joke but Tom thought it was a great idea. He got the determined look on his face he always got when he was working the numbers in his head and Jennifer had to admit to herself she loved that look. Eight months later, the mini mall had a grand reopening. The parking lot was packed, and the convenience store owner, who had been so impressed he took the suite next door as well, and the three other new tenants were very happy. Jennifer and Tom were happy, too. Tenants for the last four spaces were lining up, and the investment, the best of both their worlds, was really going to pay off.

Tip: Just as you can refurbish houses, you can refurbish other kinds of properties and either sell them or lease them, as appropriate.

1. Remember, above all, that if a mini mall or other retail establishment is in disrepair, it means the property did not make money for the owners. That may be a reason to consider whether or not it is the location and not the property's condition that is the problem.

2. While a number of novices gain experience fixing up houses, commercial properties are probably best saved for investors who have already done some property refurbishing.

3. Remember that just like renting homes, renting retail space is all about the tenants. They are your customers and the better value they get, the more loyal they will be.

Petra and Gunther and the Warehouse

The old warehouse had stood empty for as long as Petra could remember, and she had grown up just a few miles from its location so that meant at least twenty-five years. Gunther decided to look into it and he learned the old warehouse belonged to an insurance company, an asset they owned and evidently forgot about. He called a real estate agent and asked her to investigate for him. He was pretty sure there had to be something that could work. When the real estate agent got back to him, he explained that the property was owned by an insurance company. It had been purchased years before and just remained on their list, a non performing asset. The real estate agent told him the company indicated they would be willing to entertain an offer. Gunter thought it was highly possible they could divide the warehouse into suites with an office in front and a workshop or warehouse space in back. He made a quick sketch and brought it to the city. They were fine with the idea so he made an offer. It was a very low offer but he knew this property meant nothing to the company who owned it. So, he was only a little surprised when they accepted! A year later, there was an import business, a rowboat manufacturer, a wholesale game broker and an appliance repair company. They were confident the other three spaces would be leased soon as well. It was turning out to be a profitable investment but to Petra the best part was that it would actually be useful again.

Tip: Oftentimes, buildings are neglected because the owner is not motivated to create anything of value there. These can represent tremendous opportunities.

1. Financial funds like insurance companies and pension management often own properties and after many years they have already earned more than they want and have enjoyed the tax benefits.

2. Sometimes, simply thinking about the market and how a property might benefit the market will be enough to locate and act on opportunities that come up like Petra's warehouse.

3. When you pay attention to how real estate works, it helps you to see the potential opportunities. Live a life of constant learning.

Willy and Violet and their Own Factory

Violet did not know what injection molding was. Oh, she had a general idea of what it created but she did not know how any of it worked. So, when she saw a building for sale and told Willy they ought to see if there was an opportunity there, it did not really matter to her that the building used to be an injection molding factory. The two of them had purchased a great many properties and she loved the location but this would be the first time they bought anything industrial. Willy did some research. The property had been vacant for six years but the manufacturing company was still under lease and paid rent. The rent would go away in seven months, though, and it did not seem like the owners had any real interest in keeping the property afterward. He enlisted the aid of a real estate agent, and the agent contacted the owners. The next day he and Violet took a look. It was mostly wide-open space with a concrete floor except for offices along one wall and on a second story along that wall. She did not know what they could do with it but Willy had an idea. He had just bought a car and knew the dealership wanted to relocate. He thought the location would be perfect. And he was right! In just a few months, modifications were made and within four months, there were luxury cars there! Violet loved the way it all worked out and the car dealership could not be happier. Willy thought it just went to show that all it takes is a little vision to make something work.

Tip: Repurposing buildings is very common today as areas change in terms of need, opportunity and political climate. Here are some thoughts.

1. With today's common open-office settings, almost any building can become an office. Working with planning departments with local governments can often lead to opportunities.

2. Just as Willie and Violet turned this into a showroom, working with an auto dealer, there are often opportunities to modify a property if you find the right tenant.

3. Although thinking creatively can be exciting, remember you do not want to force a deal that does not make sense. That is a quick way to end up frustrated and unhappy.

Gwendolyn and Gregory and the Old Hotel

The hotel looked like something out a movie, a travel lodge from Hollywood's golden age. It was quirky and fun but it had clearly fallen on bad times. It was empty except for a big plywood "for sale" sign. That was not all that surprising given that the highway no longer went by the hotel. The highway was twenty miles to the east now, and that explained why a motor inn just did not make much money. Still, there was plenty of civilization! The entire area was growing, and even if a hotel was out of place here, it seemed woeful and wasteful that it should just be left to fall apart. They got an agent to do some research and were able to find the owners of the property. They toured the thirty-two rooms and Gwen had an idea. What if they converted the rooms to little studio apartments? She thought it would cost about four or five thousand dollars per room to add a kitchenette and do some basic renovation. The property was priced very low, basically just the value of the land. If there was a market for thirty-two studio apartments, though, this would be an excellent opportunity. They did their research, and the more they did the more excited Gwen got. In the end, they bought the property and they ended up with thirty-one apartments and used the other for a laundry room. The numbers looked great and the stack of rental applications told them they had made a great decision.

Tip: Sometimes, the opportunity in a property is really hidden and it takes really thinking outside of the box to make something work. If it makes sense, though, it can be a great idea.

1. Many cities had well-considered plans for development that turned out to be ineffective. These zoning "errors" can often present opportunities for a creative investor.

2. Sometimes, a property is left in disrepair simply because it is difficult to see what to do with it. Just like Gwen saw studio apartments where others saw a motel; you can train yourself to see what might be. Try it and you will be surprised at what you can come up with.

3. Remember to check your plan against the numbers and research just like Gwen did. If the numbers do not work, do not do the deal!

Constance and Jaime Think about the Future

When they looked at the apartment building, they could understand why it was priced so low. It was a beautiful building but the builders had clearly misunderstood the market. This was clearly designed to be a luxury apartment building and this area was not the kind of area where luxury apartments would be a good investment. The place was built three years ago and the sale price suggested they would not even break even on the building costs. In fact, it was now priced appropriate for the area. There were sixty-eight apartments and only nine were rented. By Jaime's estimate, the place cost the owners thousands of dollars per year! They made an offer and when the property was theirs, they made some immediate changes. That included selling off all the expensive, high end appliances and replacing them with more moderate ones. They sold all of the granite countertops on the vacant apartments and replaced them with synthetic. They sold the expensive chandelier lights to a builder and replaced them with moderate ceiling fans. They sold off some of the fancy lawn sculptures in the common area courtyard and put up some barbecues and picnic tables. The tenants started rolling in and Jaime and Constance realized this was the first time they had ever made a property less luxurious to make it attractive. They knew the market, though, and it worked!

Tip: As sad as it might be to say, oftentimes the mistakes of other real estate professionals provide an opportunity for you.

1. Sometimes, you can solve an owner's problem by allowing them to get out of a losing property which could be a winner for you. The key is making sure the number's work.

2. Often, we think of adding something to a property to make it work but sometimes the key is making a property less of a luxury choice to better fit the market.

3. Remember how important curb appeal can be. Too fancy is oftentimes just as bad as uninviting when it comes to attracting renters.

Christina and William Go Uptown

When Christina suggested they look into some buildings on Eleventh Street, William was skeptical. It was a rundown area of town. There were not many businesses still in the area and it seemed like a bad idea in general. Christina pulled out a map and showed him some trends over the last few years. She showed how redevelopment and new construction had gradually pushed toward Eleventh. She was certain in a few years there would be new supermarkets and other businesses located there. William still felt skeptical because they always invested when there was already a market and never because they believed the market would show up there. Christina went over their portfolio with him. She told him she did not want to change how she invested in general but it would be okay to put one or two speculative properties into the mix, would it not? He made sure they could afford to handle the cost of a mortgage if the investment did not work out and then agreed to give it a shot. Boy was he glad he did! Christina was spot on in her estimates and when a developer asked to rent the bottom floor as an office, they learned he was already planning a number of renovations. It turned out the investment was not as speculative as they thought!

Tip: A riskier kind of real estate investment in speculation about neighborhood trends and property changes. It can lead to losses so you need to be careful but when it is successful, it is usually very lucrative.

1. Remember that you should never invest in a property if you could not afford to maintain the financing costs without any help from rents. This goes double for a speculative investment.

2. It is a good idea to think of investing in property just like investing in stocks or bonds. Diversification is a good thing and some amount of high risk/high reward investing can be a good thing.

3. Speculative investing is NOT gambling. Do not allow yourself to treat it like you might a lottery ticket. Make informed decisions while understanding the risks.

Bunny and Isaac and the Education Cooperative

Bunny and Isaac had been together for almost fifteen years and they loved each other very much. They worked very hard to achieve financial stability, and when they got there, they noticed a great many of their friends brought them "opportunities" and "needs." They were graceful and tried not to be hurt. When one of their oldest friends came to them and asked for some advice, they were pleased he wanted actual advice and not money. For years he had gathered around himself people interested in education for adults, people who offered classes on a limited basis. He had come up with the idea of creating a cooperative that would be sort of like an extended education center. People might learn to play piano there or they might learn how to make flat bread. He called it "artisan education." The advice he wanted was for them to review his investment plan before he presented it to a charity foundation in search of funding. They were happy to do that, and they were actually really pleased with the opportunity. They liked what he had planned and they got an idea. They had a building in their portfolio. The tenant was leaving in three months. They took him there and told him that even though his budget for a lease was much smaller, they would donate the difference every month to his charity. He was overjoyed, of course, and a year later when they visited the cooperative and saw all the learning taking place; they knew they made the right decision.

Tip: Sometimes buying a building because you have a tenant ready to go is a fantastic idea, especially if there are special circumstances that give you confidence on the tenant.

1. In some circumstances, letting a charity rent at a discounted rate can count as a charitable contribution.

2. There are a great many non-profit and for-profit organizations and these groups are organized in many ways, not just the standard corporate forms you might be familiar with.

3. Remember. Like any other deal, do not force it to make it work. Forcing deals inevitably leads to losses and bad experiences.

Sometimes It Feels Like Karol and Fred Have One Heart!

People said that about the two of them all the time because they always seemed like they were on the same page. They were the cutest couple and after fifteen years of marriage they still seemed absolutely devoted to each other. It was really special and they loved that so many of their friends noticed how they felt about each other. They imagined the fact they saw eye to eye probably explained why they were always on the same page when it came to finances and investing. They certainly saw eye to eye when it came to investing. In fact, it seemed like whatever Karol saw in a property was evident to Fred as well. When a real estate agent showed Karol a property, she immediately thought it would be perfect for a dog boarding kennel. The agent was surprised at the thought because to him it was just an empty and small warehouse. Fred arrived late and the first thing he said when he saw the building was, "Someone should put a dog kennel here." The agent was mystified but that was just Karol and Fred! The real estate agent was mystified but six months later when there were happy sounds of barking and lots of tails wagging, he had to admit the two of them had made it happen. As for Fred and Karol, they were happy. Both of them knew it would work and it did.

Tip: If you plan to invest as part of a team, there are some ground rules you will want to put in place to make sure your investments do not have a negative impact on your relationship.

1. Clear documentation about roles, decision making, and ownership is absolutely critical. Put it on paper! It will make it easier to sort out any conflicts or problems.

2. If you and your partners always seem to agree about everything, you may want to occasionally get a disinterested party to take a look as well.

3. Do not be discouraged if others do not share your vision. Listen to what they have to say but do not think that someone's faith in you is required!

Tracy and Ramona Love the Park

Tracy and Ramona really enjoyed their neighborhood but they were a little sad that there was not a park within walking distance. Once or twice a week, they would drive five miles to take the kids to a park to play. How much more convenient it would be to walk! When Ramona noticed a for sale sign on a big, empty lot, she shook her head and wondered why the city would not just buy it and make it a park. Tracy said they could buy it and make it a park. Why not? After all, they knew of a day care center looking for a new location. They might be able to build a day care center and the rent could pay for the upkeep of a small playground and landscaping. They went to the city to ask if they could do it. The city told them they could make the park but it would have to be maintained by them. There were also some liability issues involved so they would need to make sure they had a certain minimum level of insurance. There was a lot to consider but in the end the numbers made sense. Even with the expense of the park, they would still make a little bit of a cash flow. They talked to the folks at the day care center and they said they would be happy to rent the location on a long-term lease. Eight months later there was the sound of children's laughter on that big lot. Some of it came from the daycare center and some of it came from the kids playing on the jungle gym. There was a lot of laughter for Tracy and Ramona, too. When they drove by the property or brought their kids there to play, they got to know that they had made it happen!

Tip: Sometimes, investing in properties also gives you an opportunity to do something wonderful for the community. Here are some things to consider.

1. Some people choose a percentage of their monthly cash flow from properties and give the cash to charities that are important to them.

2. Some people develop amenities for neighborhoods. This requires coordination with local government so be sure you include that in any plans.

3. Some people get a lot of joy out of taking properties that are overgrown or eyesores and improving the neighborhood simply by doing something with them!

Amber and Hector and the Extra Lots

When Amber and Hector saw the house, they were really excited. It seemed perfect for them and they knew their children would love the neighborhood. With a great park right across the street, they knew the kids would always have fun things to do. If there was one thing that did not make too much sense, though, it was that the land was really irregularly shaped. They could live with that, though, because the house was everything they wanted. They owned a few rental properties so they had some experience and planned to rent out their old home. When they took possession of the house, they were amazed to learn their lot was actually four lots! There were four different assessor's parcel numbers! It took them a while to realize what that meant. They could build four more houses! In the end, they decided on keeping one lot and making it part of their backyard. They partnered with a contractor and built on the other three lots, though, and it was wonderful as the rents started flowing. They had no idea when they bought the property they would be able to do something so involved. Now, three families had a place to live because of them! It felt even more wonderful than the monthly cash flow.

Tip: You would be amazed at how many times a property is purchased and then nothing is ever done with it. This can represent a great opportunity for you.

1. Oftentimes, a purchase like the one Hector and Amber made occurs. Here, they bought for one purpose and discovered something extra. Take advantage when that happens!

2. These kinds of opportunities sometimes fall right into your lap. On the other hand, a skilled listing agent will usually be aware of the possibilities and make them known as part of the advertising.

3. Remember that real estate is an ongoing process and you are sure to be more successful when your eyes are always open for the opportunities that might come up.

Investing in Development

Rodolfo and Yesinia Buy Some Dreams

Yesinia said if they bought the land it would be like buying a dream because they could use that land to create whatever they came up with. That was a beautiful thought, and Rodolfo analyzed it all from a financial perspective. The land was seventy-three acres in size with one very large parcel and three smaller parcels. Since the smaller parcels were right against a major thoroughfare, Rodolfo thought it made sense to sell them. It would get them some cash back right away but it would also probably bring the utilities closer for their own development later. They put the three parcels up separately and though they were confident they would sell, they did not expect to have one parcel in escrow within a week! Soon, there were plans for eight houses on that parcel and that meant utilities would be connected at the street level to their own property. They made a deal with the buyer to get the other two smaller lots at a discount and he jumped at the chance. In a year and a half, there was a gas station, a strip mall and a small apartment building. Yesinia and Rodolfo went to the developer and offered them the chance to develop the large parcel in partnership with them. They worked out the details and it went wonderfully! It took almost four years to finish it all but by the end, there was an entire neighborhood where just dirt had been before! As for Rodolfo and Yesinia, instead of money as their end, they kept fourteen houses free and clear and made them available for rent. All in all, the project indeed was like a wonderful dream!

Tip: If you buy a piece a land, you really are buying the ability to build whatever you can dream up, limited only by zoning requirements and practical considerations.

1. Remember that there are usually zoning requirements that will influence what you are permitted to build.

2. How close utilities are to your land will impact the cost to build. Although most municipalities allow septic tanks and wells, nearly none would allow a house without electric service.

3. Some people will choose to develop land but keep some of the buildings for regular cash flow so you may want to consider that as a possibility for you.

Gordon and Mitsy Envision the Valley

When they saw the land, the decided to buy it simply because Gordon had it in his mind to try another small business and he thought the land would be a great place to keep ostriches. Like many of his ideas, ostrich farming never got off the ground. So, Gordon and Mitsy had a hundred acres of land right at the edge of town. It was surrounded on three sides with hills, making an attractive valley that would, unfortunately, never contain ostriches. Gordon decided he would raise goats instead and Mitsy suggested they look at other options. The land had been every inexpensive, only sixty dollars per acre, so Mitsy knew it would not take a great deal to break even or to turn a profit. It was a bit outside of the main commerce areas but she decided she would make the city planning department her first stop. She was delighted to see that the land was zoned for single family homes. They could build a total of ten and there was enough road frontage that they could do a very simple map to have the land subdivided. Gordon ran the numbers. The utilities were already at the street. Ultimately, just doing the map meant they could sell the lots to a builder. They could sell ten acre lots at a very, very attractive price well below the market and still make a great deal of money because they bought the land for such a low price. It was an obvious path, and it turned out just like they had planned... almost. They decided to build their dream house on one of the lots. It really was a beautiful house and Gordon and Mitsy probably loved it even more because the sale of the other nine lots paid for it completely!

Tip: Raw land can be scary because there is not a clear direction for development. However, in many cases that means the opportunities are not limited.

1. A trip to the local planning department will help you see what the land can be and start giving direction to your thoughts.

2. While land off the beaten path will have fewer opportunities, the price is usually very attractive, which allows for profitability with creative thinking.

3. Remember to seek the advice of an expert when you take on a project. You may also want to consult with a tax advisor to see what the impact will be of an influx of money.

Mr. and Mrs. Miller Subdivide

When they bought the home, they just loved the house. The fact that it was placed on twenty-five acres of land was beside the point. One day, when he went to the city planning department to get information about adding a brick fence Mr. Miller was surprised to learn the land was zoned for quarter acre lots. He had always assumed the land was exactly how it was zoned. He went home with the information in hand and he and his wife talked. The Millers had never backed down from a challenge and they always tried to do the best with what they had. Their lot was not just one house with an enormous back yard! It could be a hundred houses! The decided they did not want to go that far. Thy decided instead they would like acre lots or close to an acre. The Millers drew a quick sketch and they figured it would be beautiful. They brought the sketch to the city and the planning department told them they might want to hire a civil engineer to help. They hired one and he helped them see how the streets would have to be arranged, how the drainage would have to work and how the lots would be laid out. With all of those things, there was only room for eighty-seven houses but it was still a very profitable opportunity. They were excited to get to work and they were happy they had a person with development experience to guide them through the process because it made all the difference in the world.

Tip: Sometimes development is very easy because all of the utilities and street improvements are already in place. Here are some things to think about.

1. When a piece of land is zoned for single family homes, the zoning is usually expressed as lots per acre. Sometimes four lots (or single-family homes) per acre would be classified as R4, meaning Residential 4(per acre.)

2. An engineer can help you with planning including the necessary streets, the grading plans and the required water plans.

3. Sometimes the best plan involves building below the allowable density. For example, though a property might be able to handle fifty single family homes, it may work out better from a financial standpoint to build twenty-five.

Pepper and Todd Learn about Easements

When Todd learned his church wanted to sell some land that was donated, he felt moved to buy it. He really just thought about it as a donation and while Pepper was happy about that, she took a look at the land to see what could be done with it. It turned out they could subdivide it for multifamily housing. They did not really want any big apartment buildings but after some research, he learned they could actually create lots for single family or multifamily homes. More work told them the city would allow Fifty-three lots on the land. That could be fifty-three singles, duplexes, triplexes or four-plexes. They had no idea how that would work but Todd knew a contractor, Meredith. He called her and she came over. They talked for a while and agreed to meet at the site in a few days. When they did, they were surprised to see Meredith already had a map with everything drawn on it. She designed it with mostly single-family homes except for one street of duplexes on either side. She suggested they sell the homes but keep the twelve duplexes to rent out and keep the income. Pepper and Tom talked about it that evening and called Meredith. They offered her a chance to partner with them. Meredith thought the plan was great and they went about getting the plan approved and the construction underway. Boy were the church leaders amazed when a year and a half after they purchased the land Pepper and Tom donated a house to the church!

Tip: Sometimes, partnering with one or more contractors is a great way to mitigate your risk and to create something that will last.

1. If you subdivide, and it is important to you that buildings are built, you can make sale contingent on improvement.

2. In any locality, regulations and rules about development will require compliance. Understanding these rules ahead of time will save a great deal of effort.

3. Building charitable contributions into your project is not only a very nice thing to do but it also can have some tax benefits so check with a tax advisor to see what options are available to you.

Roy and Lynne Want to Mix It Up

When they travelled across the country, Roy and Lynne loved little towns where they would see a shop with a home in the same building. Sometimes, the owners lived on top or in the back and sometimes those spaces were leased to someone else. They thought it was really neat and they decided all at once that they would try to build some in their home town. Roy built a number of houses over the course of his life, and he thought he would call some of the contractors he knew to see if they could help the process along. It was fun and a little scary all at once. The first person Roy called was the man who had built the house Roy and Lynne called home. He came over and heard their idea. He told them he was leaving town but he could help them get in the right direction before he moved in about four weeks. That was a big help and before he and his family left, he had identified seven possible lots and suggested three local contractors who could do the building. He also introduced them to the city planning officials, who told them what was necessary. There was not too much involved. They would have to get a variance that would allow the residence but they were happy to do that because to them, the empty lots did not contribute to the town at all. Roy and Lynne hired the contractor and got started. What a wonderful thing to think one of the things they loved about travelling would be right in their hometown!

Tip: Mixed use is exactly what it seems to be. It means buildings can have multiple purposes. Here are some thoughts.

1. In some large cities, you might see shopping on the first few floors and residences on higher floors.

2. Many municipalities are very happy to consider mixed use properties because of the efficiency of the property and the greater longevity of small businesses with owners living on site.

3. Remember whenever you take on a project of significant size, there are probably tax and legal implications so make sure you check with a professional.

Shelly and Miah Draw a Map

Shelly and Miah did not know anything at all about drafting or engineering. All they knew was that they had in their minds how they would like the hundred and thirty acres they inherited from their grandfather to end up. He had been a really wonderful man, and they wanted to develop the land in a way that would honor him. They figured they would have to put in a little fishing hole. Grandpa loved to fish. They thought about other things he loved. He really enjoyed playing yard games like horseshoes and the like. They would have to have horseshoe courts. Of course, they also wanted it to be a place for people to live so there would have to be houses, too. They put it all together on a map and went to the city. The city looked it over and started explaining thins but Shelly and Miah did not really understand. Eventually, the employee pointed out a bulletin board where they might find a business card from a company that could help them. They ended up speaking with a developer who helped them. They ended up with a lovely little subdivision with twenty-four homes surrounding a lovely park. They were even able to build their fishing hole! In order to make it work, they had to create a homeowner's association but that was fine by them. They knew Grandpa would be very proud of them, and what more could they ask?

Tip: There are endless possibilities when you own land although you will need to work with local government to determine what can and cannot be done according to local regulations.

1. Most cities have zoning regulations designed to ensure a good balance between housing, retail, office and other types of buildings.

2. You can certainly design a community with amenities that are important to you but there are definitely considerations you will need to address, not the least of which is whether those amenities will attract home buyers or renters.

3. The more amenities in a subdivision, the more maintenance there will need to be. This can sometimes mean a homeowner's association even if one is not ordinarily required by law.

Lupe and Gus Make a Neighborhood

Lupe and Gus always thought it would be a wonderful thing to name streets after their children. Sure, it was just idle conversation but as they grew older and there were grandkids, they really started thinking about it seriously. After all, they had been pretty successful and had the money to buy some land. How hard could it be to do something like that? They headed to a real estate agent to get a list of parcels available. It was there they got the first idea of how difficult it could be to realize their vision. There was a lot that went into a neighborhood and it would take a civil engineer to help with planning and even though they could afford to buy the land, they would have to figure out how to manage financing on the scale they wanted. After all, with the kids and grandkids, there were fourteen streets they had to name! After working with the civil engineer, they realized this was a lot more work than they were going to be able to handle on their own. The civil engineer made some phone calls on their behalf and they were able to hire a project manager and to partner with a contractor. It was still a lot of work but it was not overwhelming anymore. Lupe and Gus were thrilled. When it was all said and done, they would have a nice profit and fourteen streets named after those they loved most in the world!

Tip: For many, development of land becomes the legacy they leave behind. Therefore, they often make some of the development personal in nature.

1. Many times, you will be able to name the streets in your subdivision. Sometimes you will need to follow a plan already in place from the city.

2. Just like Lupe and Gus, sometimes it makes sense to partner with an experienced developer. There are a number of ways to manage the partnership, and that will be up to you.

3. Although some real estate projects can be very, very lucrative; you should realize that there is also a great deal of work involved.

James and Meaghan Decide on Commercial

When they bought the land, they really only bought it because they wanted to avoid bitterness in the family. Six relatives, including Meaghan, had inherited a portion of several acres of land. Meaghan knew enough about her family that there would be battles and fights because one uncle really had a problem with one of the aunts. She was not looking forward to that. James suggested they just make an offer for the whole lot so that part was settled right away. It was only a few thousand dollars per relative and they were pretty sure if they just listed it for sale, they would get their money back. When they went to a real estate agent to ask about selling it, they were surprised to discover he had been in regular communication with the great uncle who passed away and left the land to his heirs. He had been trying to get him to develop it for some time. In fact, he already had a plan in place, two actually. One involved building eighty-two homes and one involved setting up a retail and office complex. The land would work for either with the city's blessing. In the end, they decided on the retail with the office complex. They thought it would be nicer for the city to have some new services available and the location seemed very convenient for any office. When they broke ground six months later, they were really excited but that was nothing compared to when they cut the ribbon. It was just wonderful that something she did just to keep the peace turned into something so lovely!

Tip: Sometimes, properties are subject to older restrictions (or freedoms) and that can alter their value either as raw land or as developed land.

1. It is very important to check with local authorities in regard to land use in order to effectively plan for the disposition of the asset.

2. When you have a plan that you believe will work but the property is zoned in a way that makes it impossible, you can ask the city for a variance. A variance allows a property to be developed in a way that differs from the zoning.

3. Be sure to celebrate your victories. When you complete a project, you have left something wonderful for people to use and see for many, many years.

Miguel and Ellie Find an Expert

If you need to get something done right, you bring in an expert. That was Miguel's mantra, and it had served him well in business over the years. When a friend came to him with an opportunity that came from another friend, he agreed to look at it. It was land. Miguel had invested in a great deal of real estate but this was the first time he looked at raw land. He was sure he would not be buying it but he was good to his word and took a good, long look. That was when he brought in the expert. Something told him it was a good idea but he did not understand why. The expert was part of a development firm and he told Miguel the land could be developed on the south side into a small subdivision and then in the northeast into multifamily homes like four-plex townhomes and the northwest portion could be developed into a small shopping center with a grocery store and some other services. Miguel was amazed and he made an offer on the land. Then, he went back to the developer expert and offered a partnership. The deal was sealed and they got to work. There was a great deal of work, in fact, but Miguel and Ellie learned a great deal. They learned so much, in fact, that when they were finally done, they decided to take some of the profits and invest in another large parcel of land!

Tip: Cities often have a number of ideas about the best way for land to be used. Often, they will help you understand what they believe will work, and they have paid for the research!

1. Remember that every real estate project gives you the opportunity to learn. The key is to seek good quality advisors so that when you learn you do not cost yourself too much money!

2. Cities regularly seek to get certain companies to locate in their towns. Communicating with the right people at the city can offer insight and opportunities.

3. When a project is very large in scope, it often makes sense to partner with an experienced developer. This is especially helpful for the city because they will want to ensure that if a company makes plans to put a location in town the building will be completed.

Ronnette and Dale and the Entire Block

When Ronnette saw the listing for single family land, she was surprised that the price was so low. She went to investigate and it suddenly made sense. There was one half-completed house and there were four foundations. Someone had begun the process years ago but left the project unfinished. There were even roads that ended abruptly in the dirt. All of this was across the street from the lots offered for sale. She knew the property values of any homes placed on those lots would be low if things were left as they were. For most people, that would mean there was no reason to buy the lots. For Ronnette, that meant there was opportunity! She made an offer on the lots and then asked her real estate agent to find out who owned the unfinished project across the street. It turned out to be owned by the bank that loaned for the project. Naturally, Ronnette decided to see if she could acquire the project. The bank was very happy to have a buyer but Ronnette said she would only buy the land if she could see the plans for the previous project in total. The bank handed them over and she agreed to buy the land if the bank financed the project. Naturally, the bank was worried about losing even more money but Ronette was able to convince them she could get the project finished. She did, too! In fact, the bank was so happy they offered to finance her next project, too, whatever it was!

Tip: The world of development has its ups and its down and sometimes uncompleted projects can be an excellent opportunity.

1. REO departments of banks have portfolios of properties. REO stands for real estate owned. These are properties the banks own because they had to foreclose.

2. While banks usually have no trouble liquidating their completed buildings, a project early in the development process usually just stays on their books.

3. If you purchase a property from the bank that involves financing, they will need reassurance that you will complete the construction.